Directions: Find the twin pictures, and color them exactly the same.

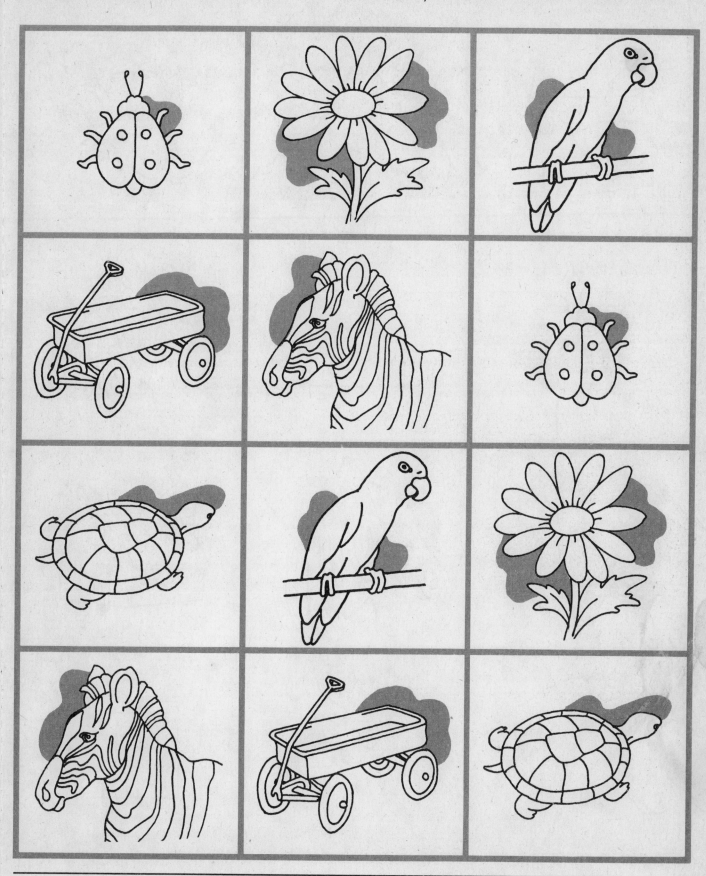

Directions: Find the twin pictures, and color them exactly the same.

Directions: Look at the letter near each dot. Draw connecting lines between the letters that look the same. Color the surprise picture.

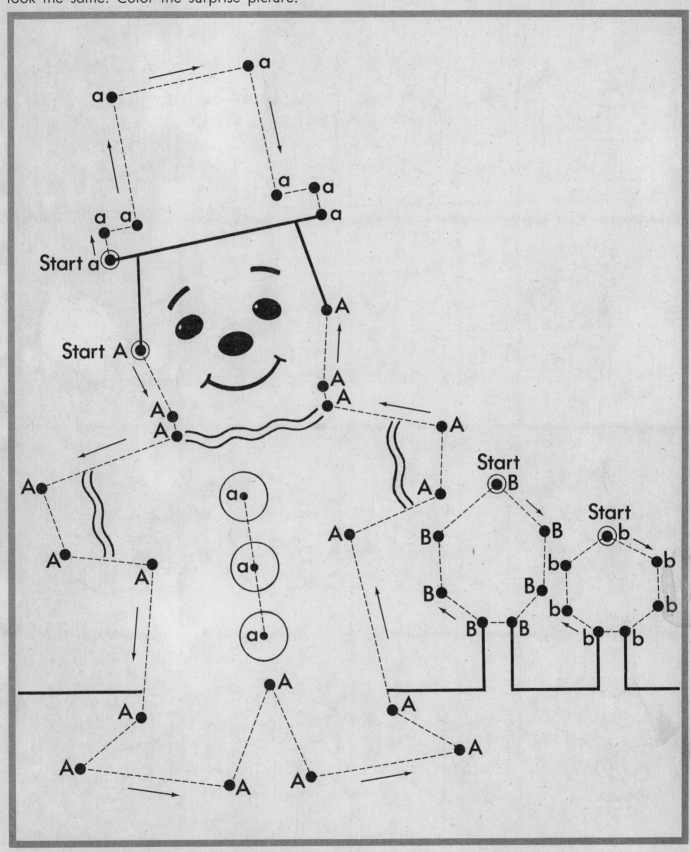

9

LESSON 3: IDENTIFYING Aa, Bb

Directions: Color the box and lid green if the letters are partners (capital and small of the same letter). Make the other boxes red.

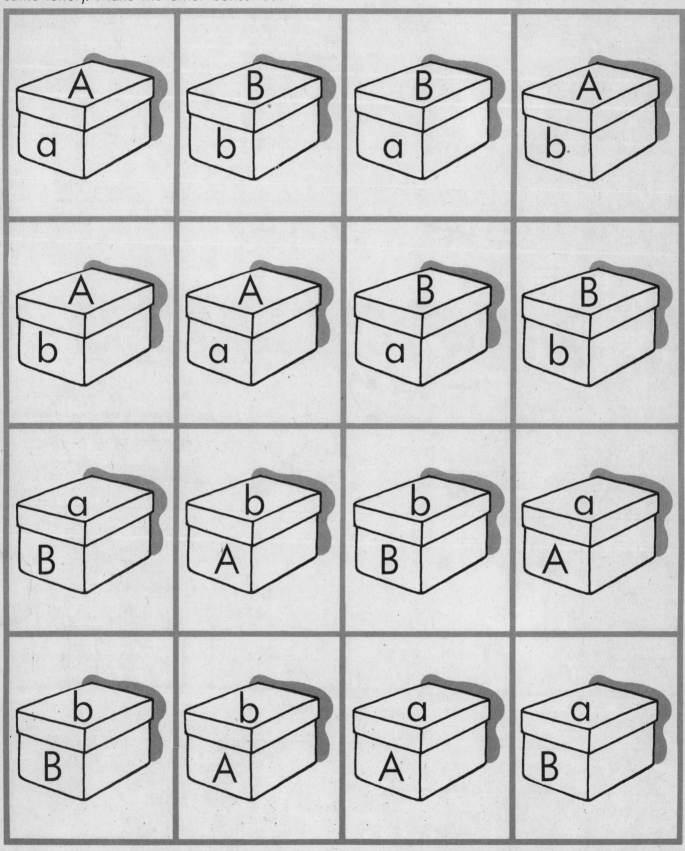

Directions: Look at the letter in the corner of the box. Find the same letter in each word, and draw a ring around it. The first one shows you what to do.

b

(b)ird
baby
rub
ribbon

c

cap
coat
rack
cow

d

dog
pedal
red
ladder

a

ax
mail
and
cane

c

coat
rock
come
cold

d

duck
deep
Ned
glad

a

apron
ask
banana
cap

b

boat
tub
rubber
bell

Directions: Look at the letter in each box. Then look at the word list, and draw a ring around each word that begins with its partner letter. The first one shows you what to do.

| a | coat (Alice) Cindy Anna |

| c | Carla Bart Carol Dan |

| b | Bill Dick Dave Bob |

| d | Beth David Don Dora |

| D | daisy doll bell desk |

| B | den berry box Donna |

| A | able cap apple and |

| C | card dart aunt cans |

| d | Dan Becky Debbie Ben |

14

Directions: Color the box red if it has the same letter as the big box at the left.

E	E	F	A	E	E
	E	E	F	E	F
e	e	e	a	e	c
	e	c	e	a	e
F	E	F	F	E	F
	F	B	F	F	E
f	f	b	f	f	d
	b	f	f	d	f

Directions: Color the box red if it has the same letter as the big box at the left.

15

Directions: Color each box that has partner letters. Color the eagle and the fox.

Emma Eagle and Freddy Fox
can find the partner letters.

Can you find them?

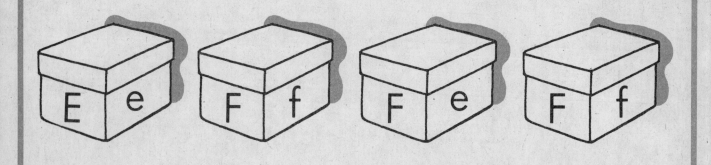

16

Directions: Draw a ring around each letter in the box that is the same as the letter in the middle.

G G **(G)** C G	h h **(h)** h b	H M **(H)** H H	e g **(g)** g g
H H **(H)** H L	a g **(g)** d g	H K **(H)** H L	h h **(h)** n k
O G **(G)** G G	g g **(g)** d p	G C **(G)** G G	H H **(H)** H L
d h **(h)** b h	Q G **(G)** G O	H L **(H)** H E	g p **(g)** g g

Directions: Color each balloon that has partner letters.

 Dan and Jane need help.

Find the partner letters for them.

gG   Go   Hk   hH

Hh   hK   Ge   Gg

Hb   Hh   gC   gG

Directions: Color the box blue if it has the same letter as the big box at the left.

I	I	J	I	E	I
	F	I	I	I	J
i	i	j	f	j	i
	i	l	l	i	i
J	I	J	J	L	J
	J	I	L	J	J
j	j	g	j	i	j
	l	i	j	J	j

19

Directions: In each box color the triangles that have partner letters. Make **Ii** one color and **Jj** another color.

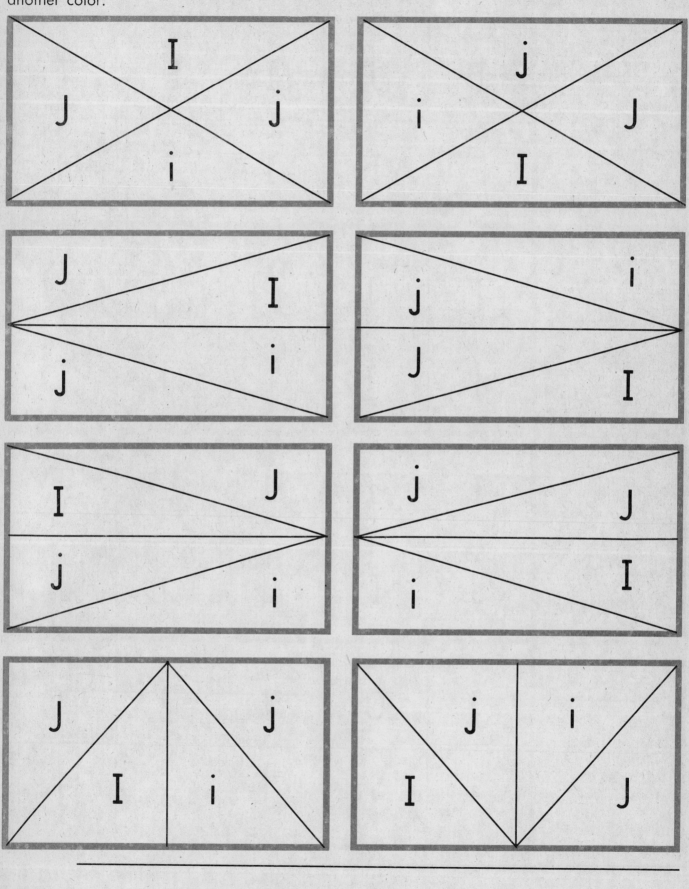

Directions: Look at the letter in the corner of the box. Find the same letter in each of the words, and draw a ring around it. Color the pictures. The first one shows you what to do.

e

k i t (e)
m e a t
e a t
e e l

f

f i s h
c u f f
f o r
f i f t y

g

g o a t
b u g
l o g
w i g g l e

h

h i s
h u s h
b e h a v e
h o w

i

m i l k
p i e
i l l
i c i c l e

j

j a m
b l u e j a y
j u m p
j a c k e t

f

m u f f
f a m i l y
f i r e
s o f t

h

h o m e
h o r s e
m u c h
a n y h o w

21

Directions: Look at the letter in the circle. Find the square that has the letter that comes after it in the alphabet. Color the circle and the square yellow.

(C)	D F G	(A)	E D B	(B)	H C E	(F)	I A G
(E)	I K F	(G)	H J C	(D)	K A E	(I)	G J H
(H)	I G K	(J)	A K I	(a)	e c b	(i)	j d h
(b)	f c a	(f)	g i k	(j)	a k d	(e)	d b f
(h)	i g e	(c)	a h d	(d)	j e c	(g)	h f i

22

Directions: Draw a ring around the letters that are the same in each box. The first one shows you what to do.

k k	L F	H K	L K
l l	L K	L K	K L
k l	K K	l k	L L
l k	L L	l k	K K
h k	K L	K L	l l
k b	L K	K L	k k
L K	k k	K F	k l
K L	h b	L L	l k

Directions: Color each kite that has partner letters.

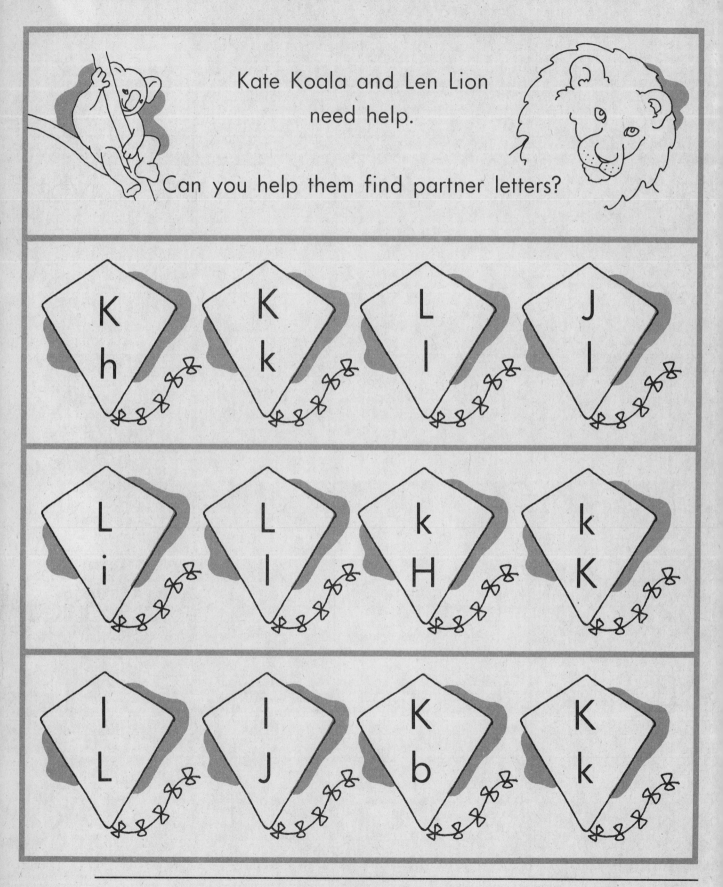

Kate Koala and Len Lion
need help.

Can you help them find partner letters?

K h	K k	L l	J l
L i	L l	k H	k K
l L	l J	K b	K k

Color each kite that has partner letters.

24

Directions: Color the box orange if it has the same letter as the big box at the left.

M	M	M	N	M	K
	M	N	W	M	M
m	m	n	m	n	n
	m	m	m	w	m
N	N	Z	N	N	N
	M	N	H	K	N
n	m	n	n	n	u
	u	n	m	r	n

Directions: Color the box orange if it has the same letter as the big box at the left.

Directions: In each box color the triangles that have partner letters. Make **Mm** one color and **Nn** another color.

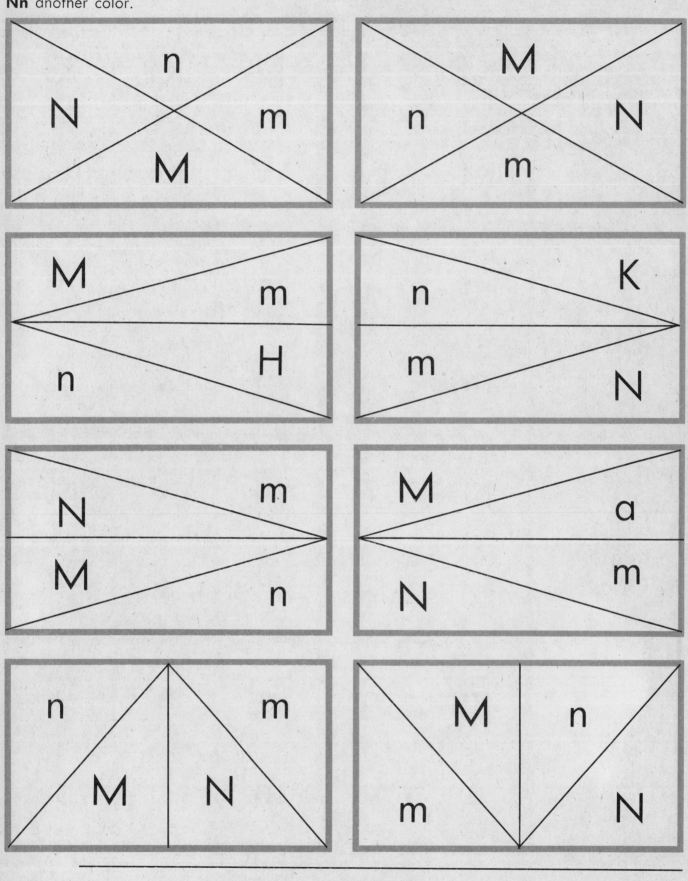

Directions: Color the box red if it has the same letter as the big box at the left.

O	O	C	O	O	G
	J	O	D	O	O
o	o	o	c	e	o
	o	a	o	o	a
P	F	P	B	P	P
	P	D	P	F	P
p	p	p	q	p	g
	b	p	p	q	p

Directions: Color the box red if it has the same letter as the big box at the left.

27

Directions: Look at the letter in each box. Then look at the word list, and draw a ring around each word that begins with its partner letter. The first one shows you what to do.

O	(on)		P	pen		o	Owen
	an			pot			Cal
	off			gull			Dan
	cat			bed			Over
	oak			phone			Ohio

p	Fran		O	end		p	Pablo
	Paul			ocean			Roy
	Pedro			apple			Philip
	Pat			open			Pam
	Bob			oven			Betty

P	pack		o	Grace		P	gate
	paint			Oz			pig
	duck			Oliver			pipe
	pole			Carla			pull
	goat			Otto			baby

Directions: Look at the letter in the corner of the box. Find the same letter in each word, and draw a ring around it. Color the pictures. The first one shows you what to do.

k  soc(k)
kitten
hike
monkey

l  lamp
taller
sail
play

m  Sam
summer
moon
lemon

n 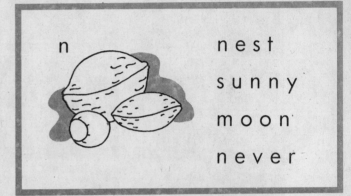 nest
sunny
moon
never

o  ox
soon
two
one

p  ripe
pan
pump
snap

n 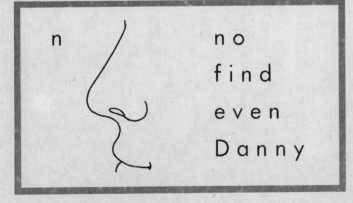 no
find
even
Danny

m  mop
jam
mother
hammer

Directions: Draw a string from the balloon to the partner letter. Then color the balloon and the box with the partner letter the same color.

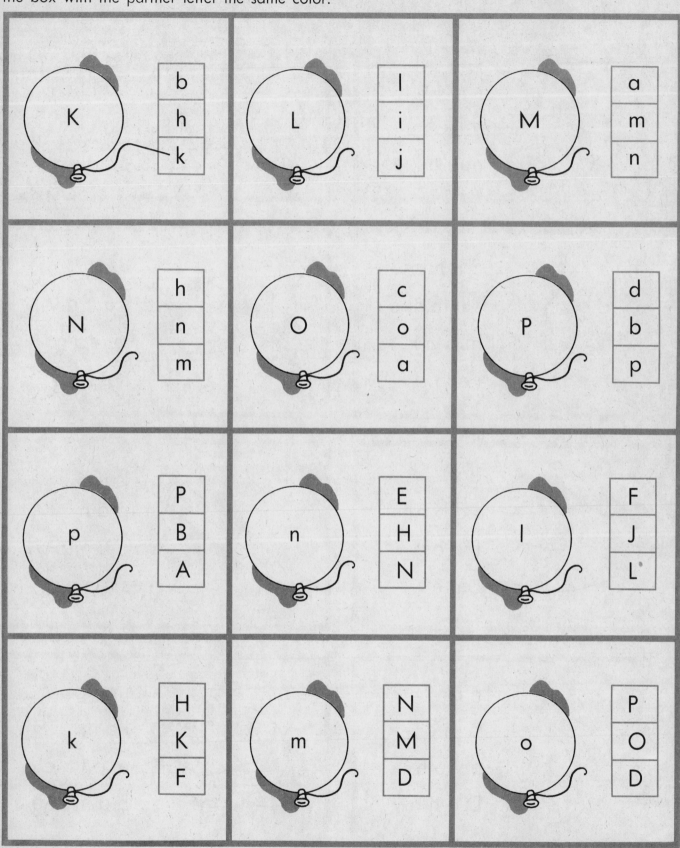

Directions: Draw a ring around the letters that are the same in each box.

Q R	Q R	R Q	R R
B Q	Q R	Q R	Q O
C Q	R B	K R	D Q
Q G	P R	H R	O Q
q q	n t	r q	q r
p g	r r	r q	r q
q g	h r	r q	g q
r q	n r	r q	q p

Directions: Look at the letter on the boat at the beginning of each row. Color each boat that has the partner letter.

Directions: Color the box green if it has the same letter as the big box at the left.

S	S	S	C	S	J
	Q	S	S	G	S

s	s	a	s	s	e
	s	s	c	m	s

T	F	T	T	T	I
	T	K	T	L	T

t	t	f	t	h	t
	k	t	t	l	t

Directions: Draw a string from the balloon to the partner letter. Then color the balloon and the box with the partner letter the same color.

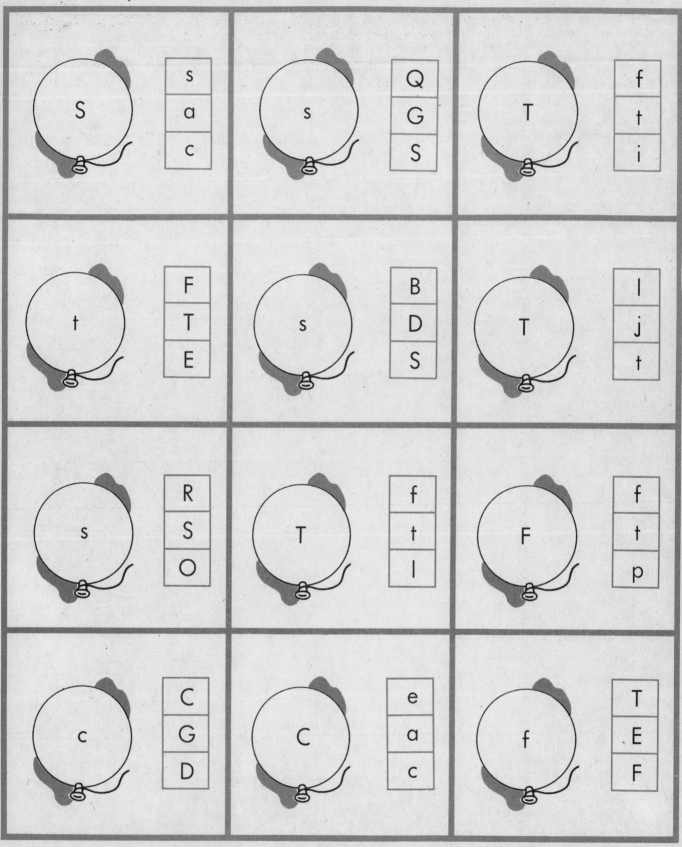

LESSON 10: IDENTIFYING U, u, V, v

Directions: Color the box yellow if it has the same letter as the big box at the left.

U	U	U	V	W	U
	C	U	U	U	J
u	u	n	u	v	u
	c	u	u	u	n
V	W	V	A	V	V
	V	K	V	L	V
v	v	v	i	j	v
	w	v	v	u	r

Directions: Color the box yellow if it has the same letter as the big box at the left.

Directions: Look at the letter in each box. Then look at the word list, and draw a ring around each word that begins with its partner letter. The first one shows you what to do.

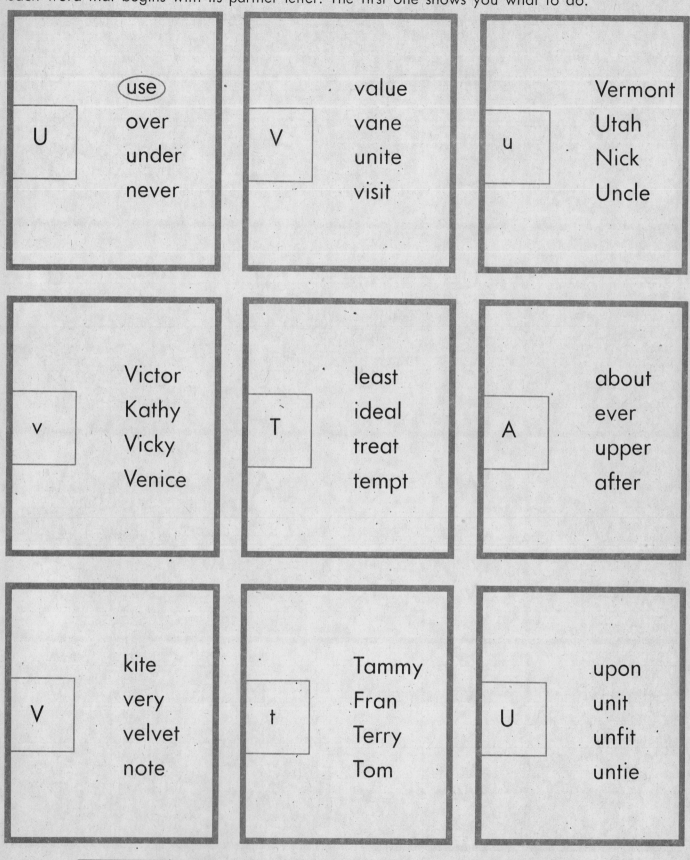

U	(use)	V	value	u	Vermont
	over		vane		Utah
	under		unite		Nick
	never		visit		Uncle

v	Victor	T	least	A	about
	Kathy		ideal		ever
	Vicky		treat		upper
	Venice		tempt		after

V	kite	t	Tammy	U	upon
	very		Fran		unit
	velvet		Terry		unfit
	note		Tom		untie

36

Directions: If the letters on the sailboat are the same, color the boat.

Directions: If the letters on the sailboat are the same, color the boat.

Directions: Color the TV if the letter on it is a partner of the letter at the beginning of the row.

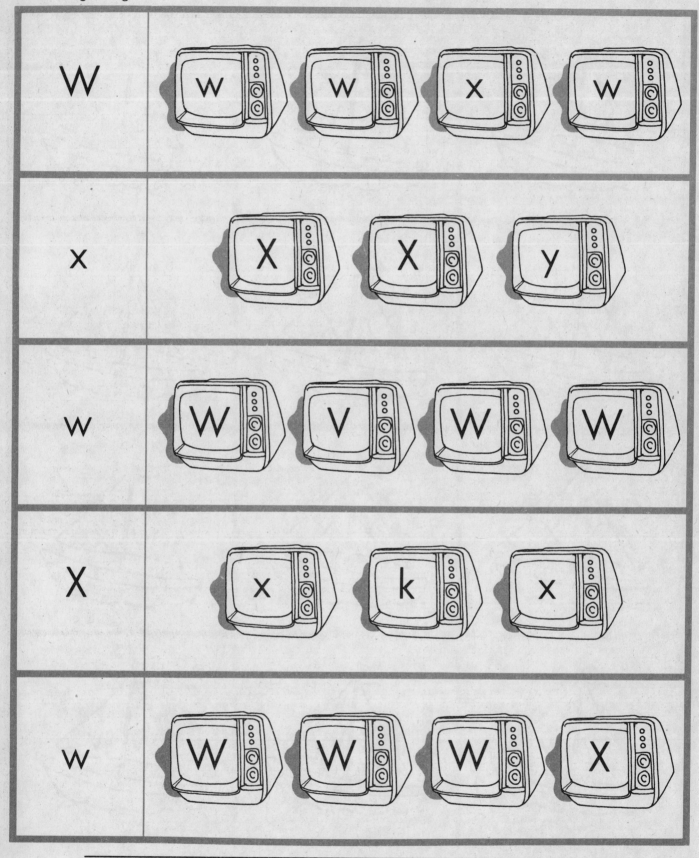

Directions: Color the box blue if it has the same letter as the big box at the left.

Y	T	Y	Y	A	Y
	Y	F	K	Y	M
y	y	t	y	k	x
	y	f	j	y	y
Z	Z	N	Z	S	Z
	W	Z	M	Z	Y
z	z	z	k	z	y
	s	z	v	z	x

39

Directions: Draw a string from the balloon to the partner letter. Then color the balloon and the box with the partner letter the same color.

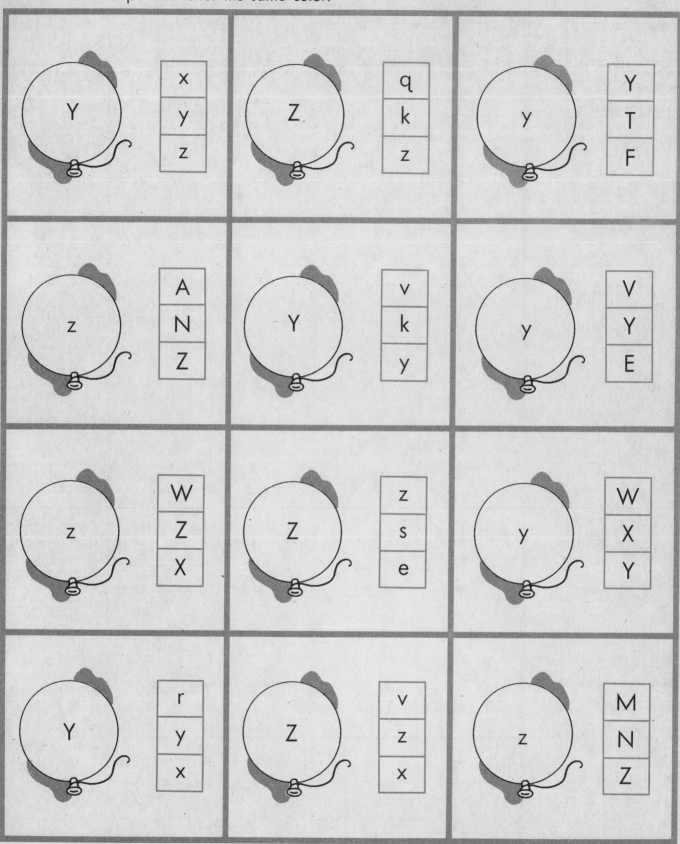

40

Directions: Look at the letter in the corner of the box. Find the same letter in each word, and draw a ring around it. The first one shows you what to do.

t		table	plant	tiger	salt	toast
t(ulip)		quit	town	rabbit	tattle	ticket
s		sister	socks	sun	sunset	snow
scissors		desk	base	safe	scrub	pass
v		vase	seven	twelve	wave	veil
violets		vest	vine	move	favor	view
r		door	ribbon	berry	tiger	garden
rabbit		runner	rabbit	grocer	rider	chair

Directions: Look at the letter in the corner of the box. Find the same letter in each word, and draw a ring around it. The first one shows you what to do.

Z		zero	zigzag	zipper	zone	zoo
(z)innia		maize	graze	fuzz	zebra	blaze
Y		yard	layer	yellow	yawn	may
yarn		yacht	maybe	silly	yes	play
X		box	taxes	fox	waxing	Max
ax		mixing	Rex	boxing	ox	ax
W		willow	warm	writer	want	wash
wagon		awake	wind	flower	water	away

42

Directions: Sun begins with the sound of **S.** Color each picture whose name begins with the sound of **S.**

Directions: Say the name of the picture. If the name of the picture begins with the sound of **S,** print **Ss** in the space below the picture.

S s

LESSON 14: RECOGNIZING THE SOUND OF T

Directions: Top begins with the sound of **T.** Color each picture whose name begins with the sound of **T.**

45

Directions: Say the name of the picture. If the name of the picture begins with the sound of **T**, print **Tt** in the space below the picture.

T t			

Directions: Ball begins with the sound of **B.** Color each picture whose name begins with the sound of **B.**

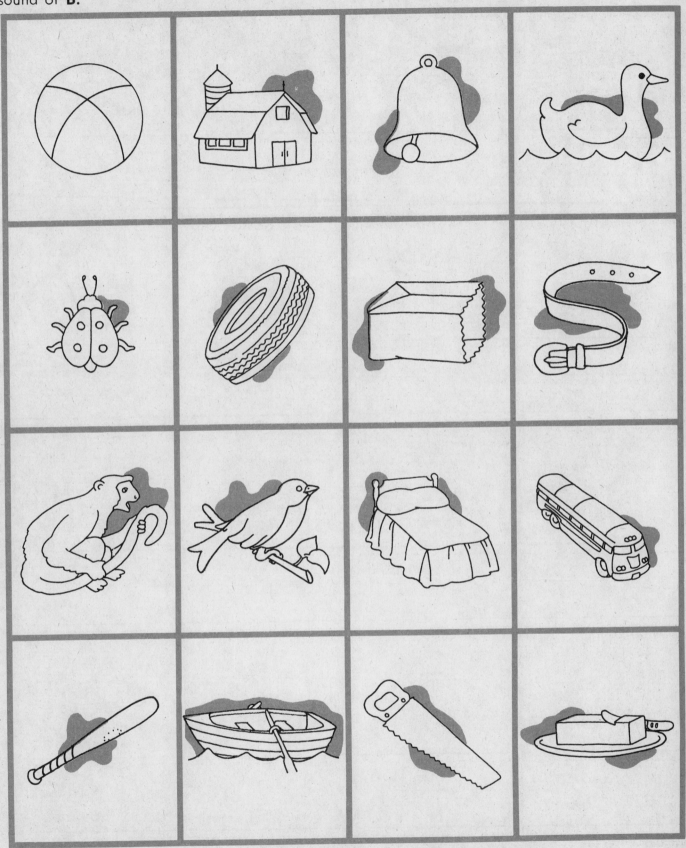

Directions: Say the name of the picture. If the name of the picture begins with the sound of **B,** print **Bb** in the space below the picture.

B b

Directions: Draw a ring around the beginning letter of the name of each picture. Color all the pictures. The first one shows you what to do.

S Ⓣ B	T B S	B S T	B T S
S T B	T B S	B S T	B T S
S T B	T B S	B S T	B T S

Directions: Say the name of the picture. If the name begins with the sound of the letter in the circle, color the left block. If it ends with that sound, color the right block.

50

Directions: Hat begins with the sound of **H.** Say the name of the picture. Draw a ring around the letter you hear at the beginning of its name. Color each picture whose name begins with the sound of **H.** The first one shows you what to do.

S
T
B
(H)

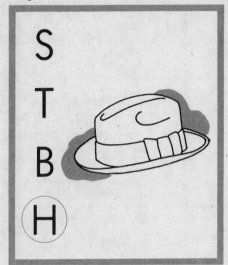

T
B
H
S

B
H
S
T

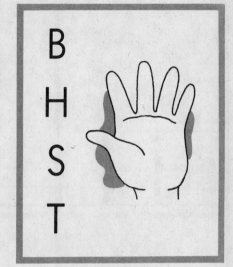

H
S
T
B

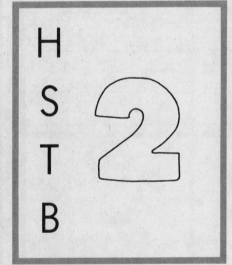

H
B
T
S

B
T
S
H

T
S
H
B

S
H
B
T

S
T
B
H

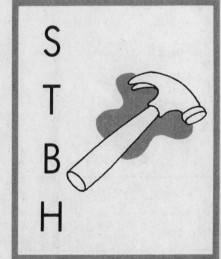

Directions: Say the name of the picture. If the name of the picture begins with the sound of **H,** print **Hh** in the space below the picture.

H h

Directions: Moon begins with the sound of **M.** Color each picture whose name begins with the sound of **M.**

Directions: Say the name of the picture. If the name of the picture begins with the sound of **M,** print **Mm** in the space below the picture.

Mm

Directions: Key begins with the sound of **K.** Say the name of the picture. Draw a ring around the letter you hear at the beginning of its name. Color each picture whose name begins with the sound of **K.**

H
M
(K)
T

M
K
T
H

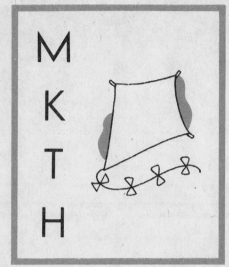

K
T
H
M

T
K
M
H

H
M
K
T

T
K
M
H

K
M
H
T

H
T
K
M

M
H
K
T

55

Directions: Say the name of the picture. If the name of the picture begins with the sound of **K,** print **Kk** in the space below the picture.

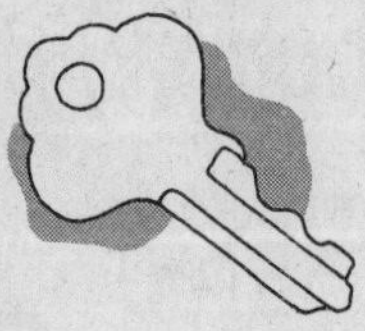

K k

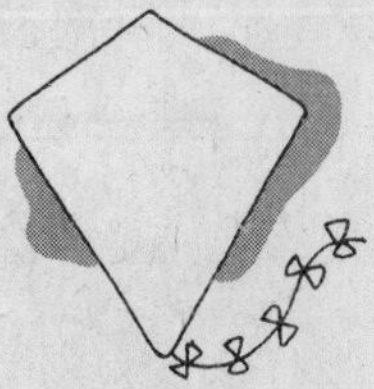

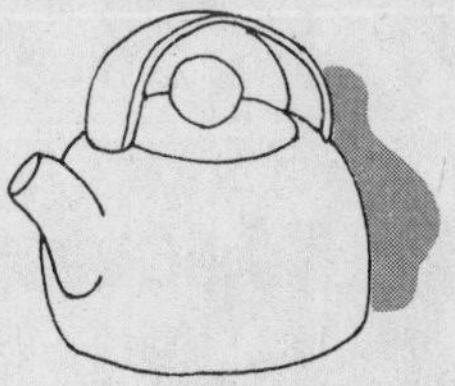

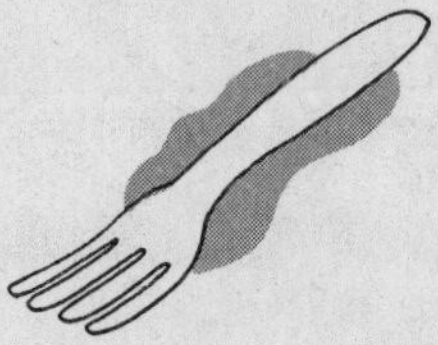

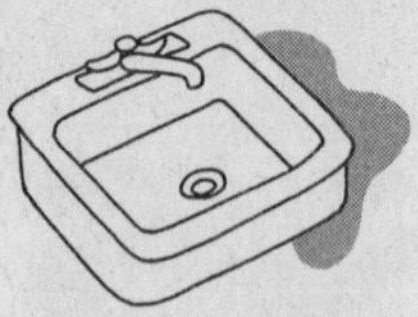

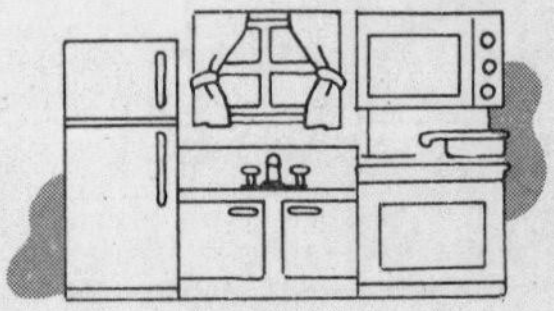

56

Directions: Say the name of the picture. Draw a ring around the letter you hear at the beginning of its name. Color all the pictures.

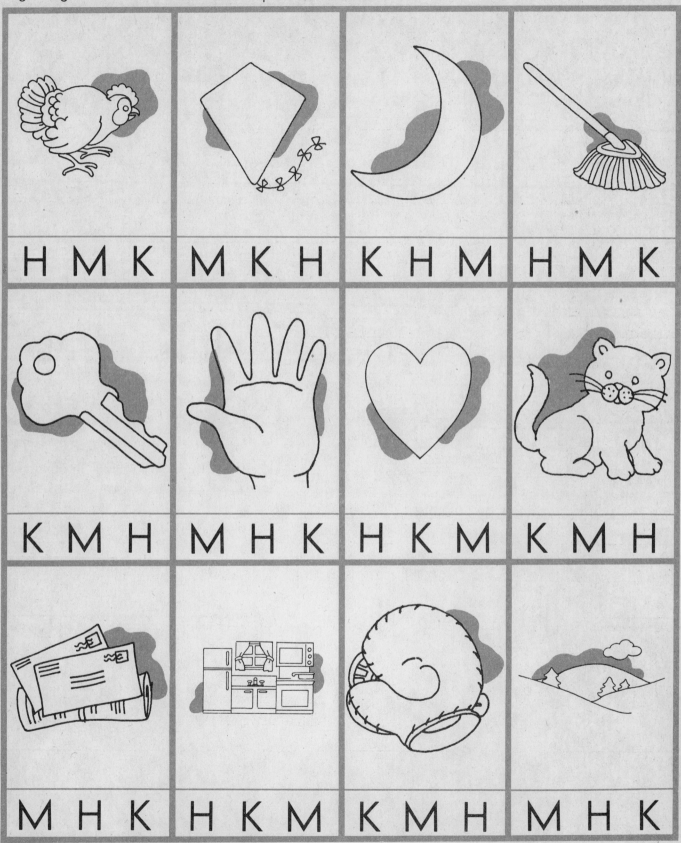

H M K   M K H   K H M   H M K

K M H   M H K   H K M   K M H

M H K   H K M   K M H   M H K

Directions: Say the name of the picture. If the name begins with the sound of the letter in the circle, color the left block. If it ends with that sound, color the right block.

m	h	m	k

k	m	h	k

h	k	m	k

Directions: In each row draw a ring around each picture whose name begins with the sound of the letter at the beginning of the row.

k	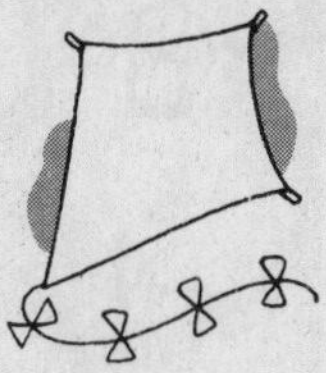	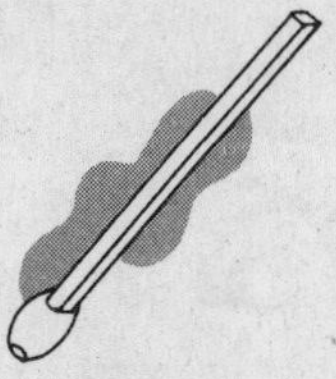	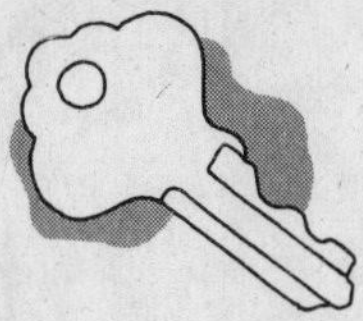	
t				
b	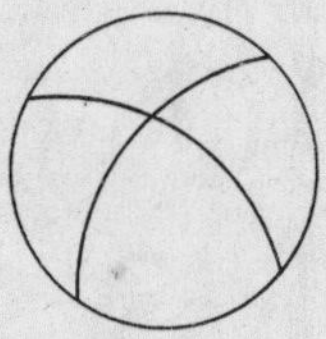			
m			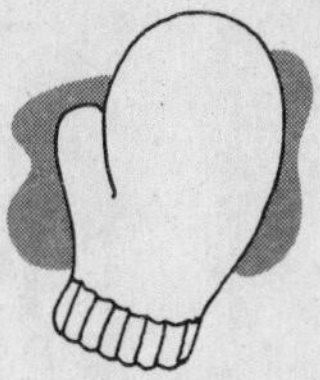	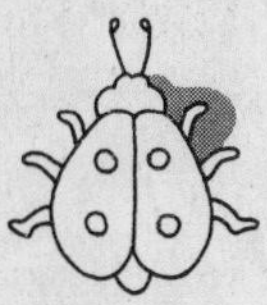
h			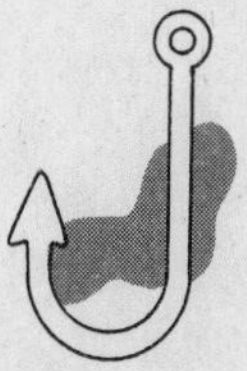	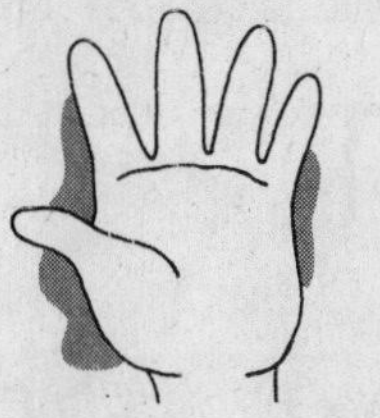
s				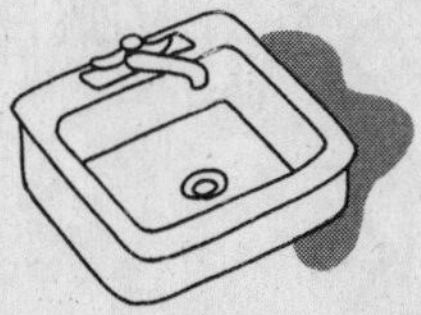

MILK

FOR SALE

Directions: Say the name of the picture. Draw a ring around the letter you hear at the beginning of its name. Color all the pictures.

S
T
B
H

M
K
S
T

B
H
M
T

T
B
M
S

H
T
K
M

K
S
H
B
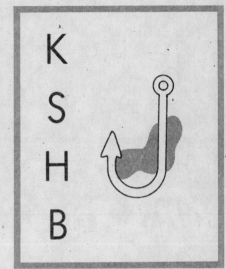

T
M
S
K

B
H
M
S

H
T
B
K

60

Directions: Jet begins with the sound of **J.** Color each picture whose name begins with the sound of **J.**

Directions: Jet begins with the sound of **J.** Color each picture whose name begins with the sound of **J.**

61

Directions: Say the name of the picture. If the name of the picture begins with the sound of **J,** print **Jj** in the space below the picture.

J j			
2			

LESSON 22: RECOGNIZING THE SOUND OF F

Directions: Fox begins with the sound of **F.** Color each picture whose name begins with the sound of **F.**

Directions: Say the name of the picture. If you hear the sound of **F** at the beginning, print **Ff** in the space below the picture. Color each picture whose name ends with the sound of **F.**

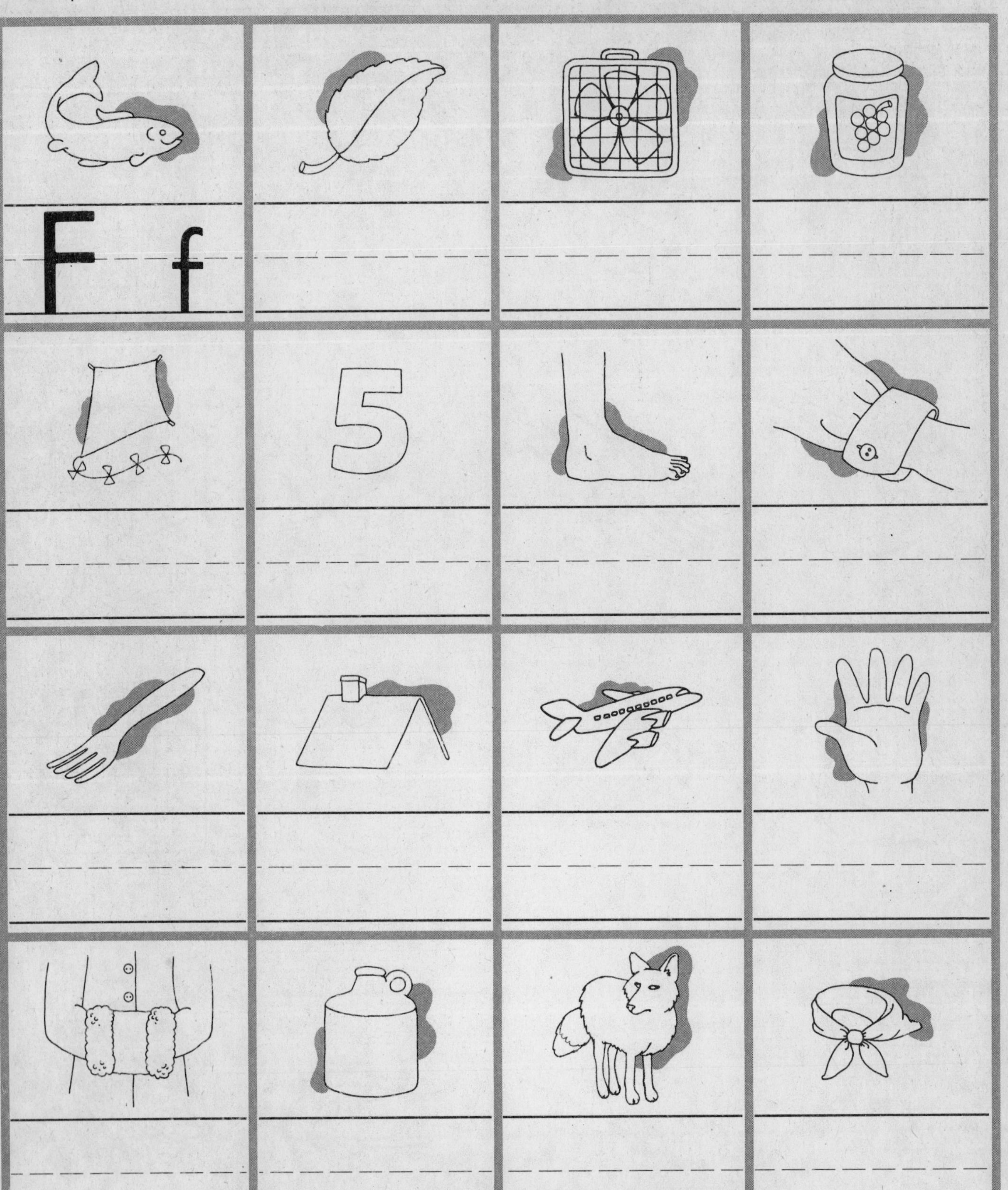

F f

64

Directions: Goat begins with the sound of **G.** Color each picture whose name begins with the sound of **G.**

Directions: Goat begins with the sound of **G.** Color each picture whose name begins with the sound of **G.**

65

Directions: Say the name of the picture. If the name of the picture begins with the sound of **G,** print **Gg** in the space below the picture.

G g

Directions: Say the name of the picture. If you hear the sound of **J** at the beginning, print **Jj** in the space; if you hear the sound of **F,** print **Ff;** if you hear the sound of **G,** print **Gg.**

67

Directions: Say the name of the picture. If the name begins with the sound of the letter in the circle, color the left block. If it ends with that sound, color the right block.

Directions: Lamp begins with the sound of **L.** Color each picture whose name begins with the sound of **L.**

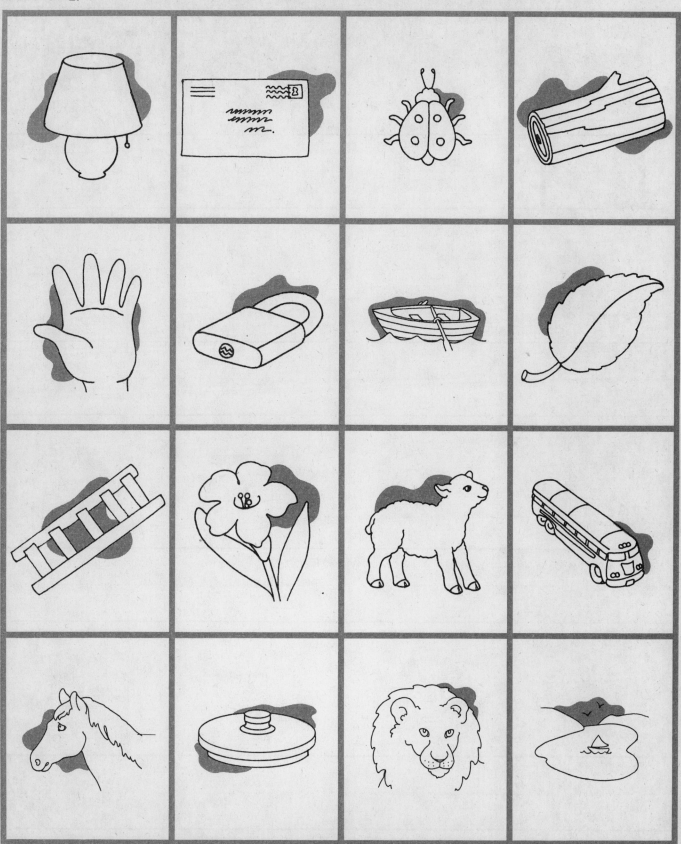

Directions: Lamp begins with the sound of **L.** Color each picture whose name begins with the sound of **L.**

Directions: Say the name of the picture. If you hear the sound of **L** at the beginning, print **Ll** in the space below the picture. Color each picture whose name ends with the sound of **L**.

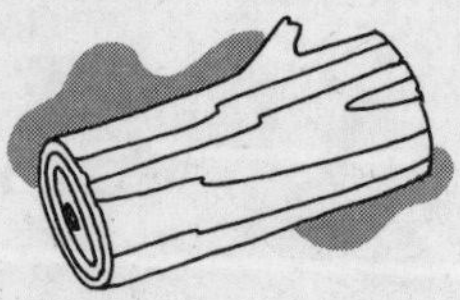

Ll

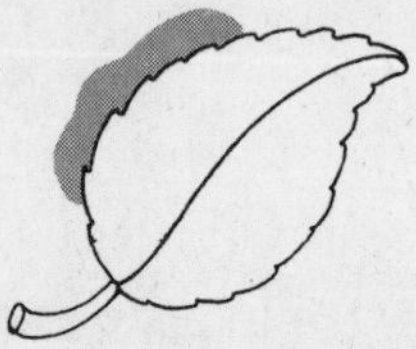

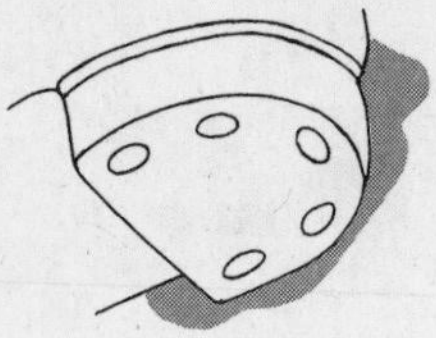

70

Directions: Dog begins with the sound of **D.** Color each picture whose name begins with the sound of **D.**

Directions: Dog begins with the sound of **D.** Color each picture whose name begins with the sound of **D.**

71

Directions: Say the name of the picture. If you hear the sound of **D** at the beginning, print **Dd** in the space below the picture. Color each picture whose name ends with the sound of **D**.

D d

Directions: Nail begins with the sound of **N.** Color each picture whose name begins with the sound of **N.**

LESSON 27: RECOGNIZING THE SOUND OF N

73

LESSON 27: RECOGNIZING THE SOUND OF N

Directions: Say the name of the picture. If you hear the sound of **N** at the beginning, print **Nn** in the space below the picture. Color each picture whose name ends with the sound of **N.**

N n

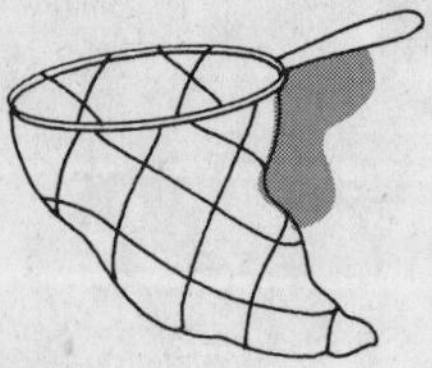

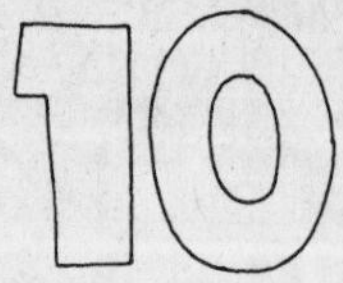

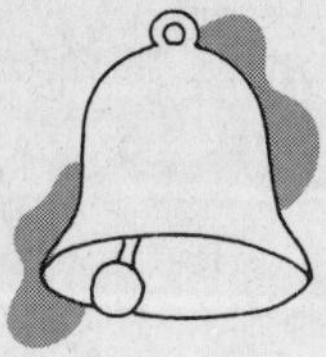

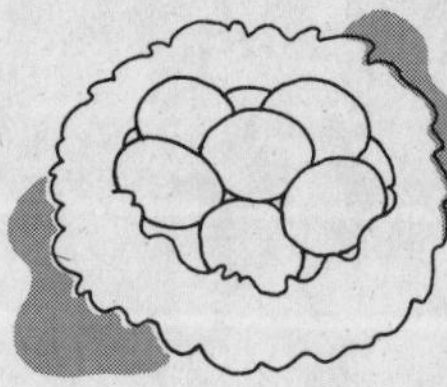

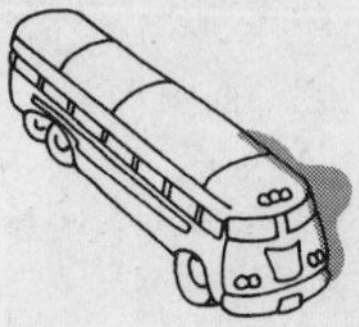

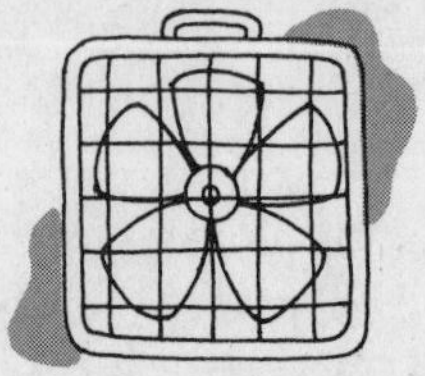

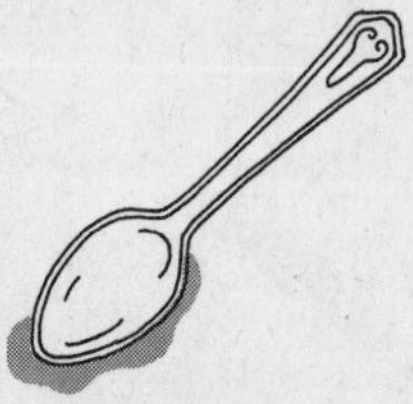

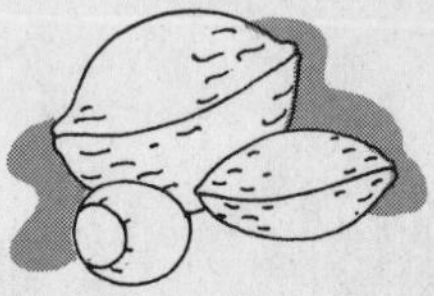

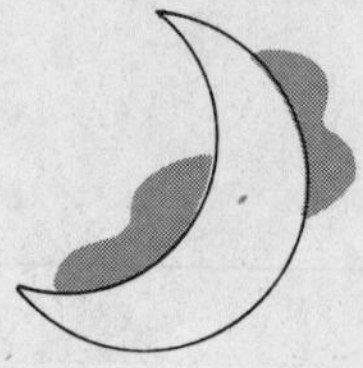

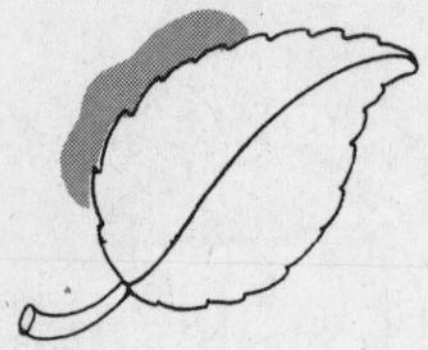

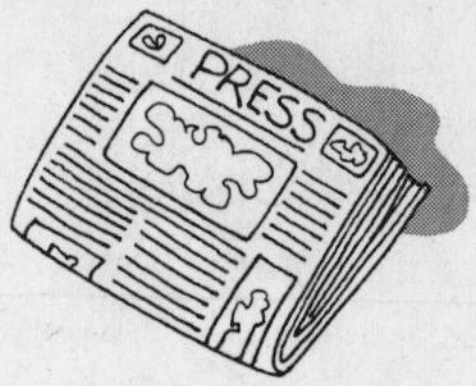

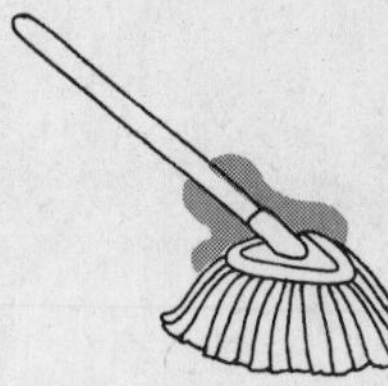

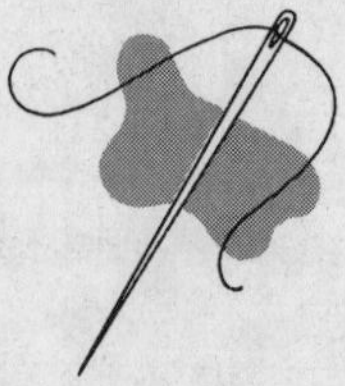

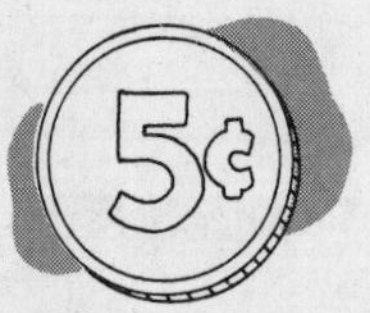

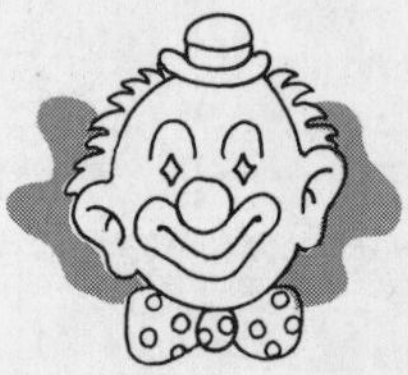

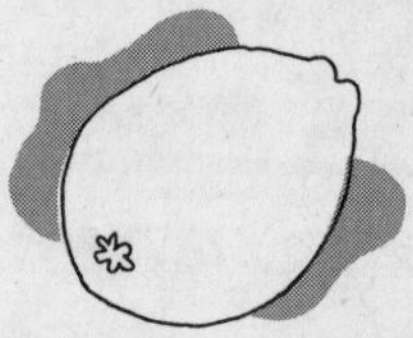

Directions: In each row draw a ring around each picture whose name begins with the sound of the letter at the beginning of the row.

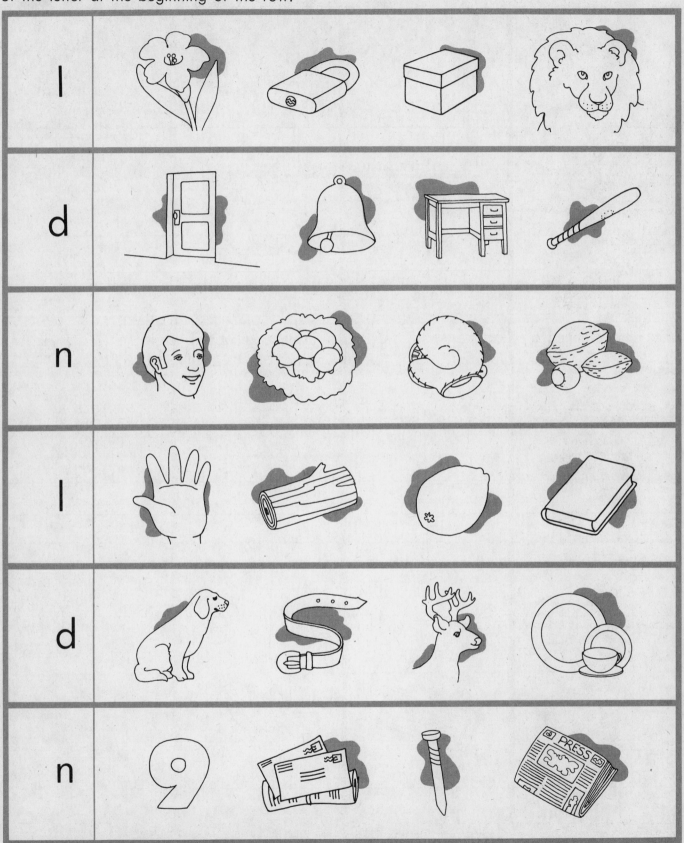

Directions: Say the name of the picture. If the name begins with the sound of the letter in the circle, color the left block. If it ends with that sound, color the right block.

ⓛ	ⓝ	ⓓ	ⓝ

ⓛ	ⓓ	ⓝ	ⓓ

ⓝ	ⓛ	ⓓ	ⓛ

Directions: Say the name of the picture. Print the letter for the beginning sound in the box at the left. Print the letter for the ending sound in the box at the right. The first one shows you what to do.

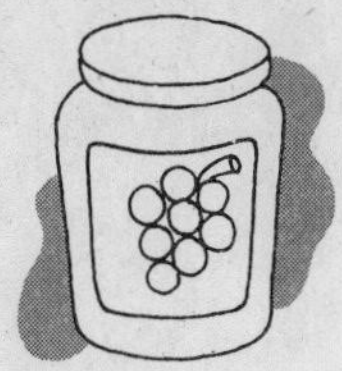

j m

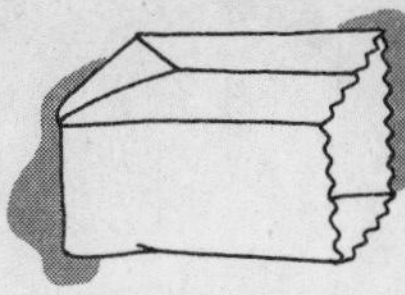

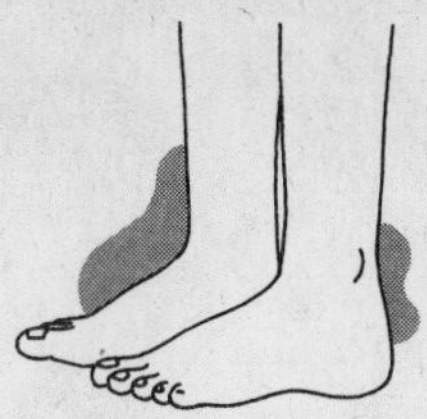

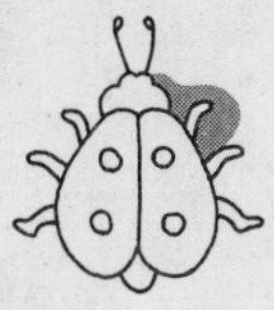

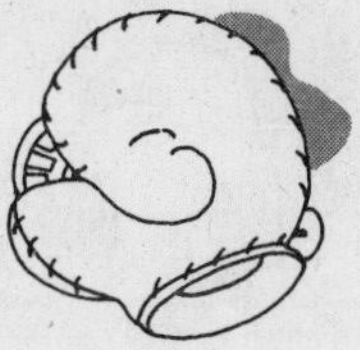

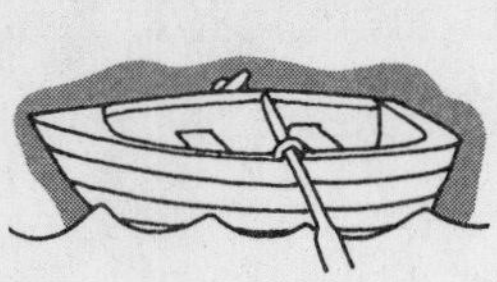

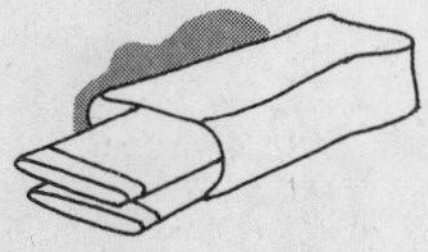

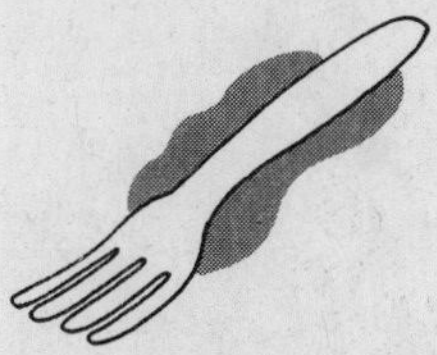

77

Directions: Say the name of the picture. Print the letter for the beginning sound in the box at the left. Print the letter for the ending sound in the box at the right. The first one shows you what to do.

s n

78

Directions: Wagon begins with the sound of **W.** Color each picture whose name begins with the sound of **W.**

Directions: Wagon begins with the sound of **W.** Color each picture whose name begins with the sound of **W.**

Directions: Say the name of the picture. If the name of the picture begins with the sound of **W**, print **Ww** in the space below the picture.

W w

Directions: Cat begins with the sound of **C.** Color each picture whose name begins with the sound of **C.**

Directions: Say the name of the picture. If the name of the picture begins with the sound of **C,** print **Cc** in the space below the picture.

Cc

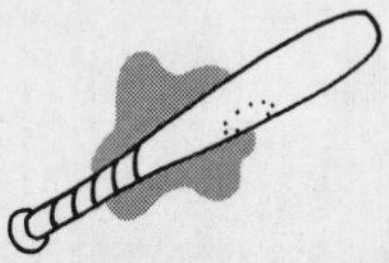

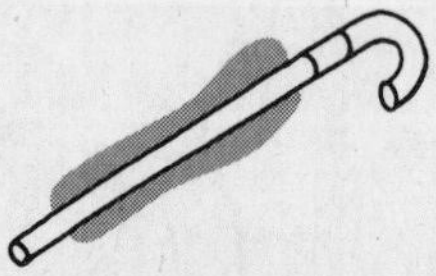

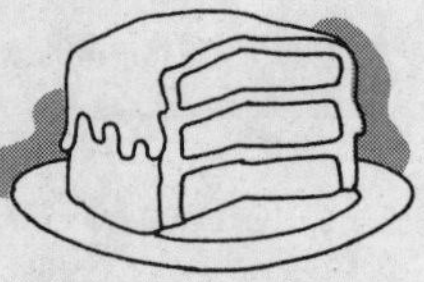

82

Directions: Rabbit begins with the sound of **R.** Color each picture whose name begins with the sound of **R.**

LESSON 31: RECOGNIZING THE SOUND OF R

83

Directions: Say the name of the picture. If you hear the sound of **R** at the beginning, print **Rr** in the space below the picture. Color each picture whose name ends with the sound of **R**.

R r

Directions: Say the name of the picture. Draw a ring around the beginning letter of the name of each picture. Color all the pictures.

W C R   W C R   W C R   W C R

W C R   W C R   W C R   W C R

W C R   W C R   W C R   W C R

Directions: Say the name of the picture. Print the letter for the beginning sound to complete the name for each picture.

eaf	ake	ope	ell
esk	ine	et	one
oad	ing	ar	eer
up	ock	ock	eb

Directions: Pig begins with the sound of **P.** Color each picture whose name begins with the sound of **P.**

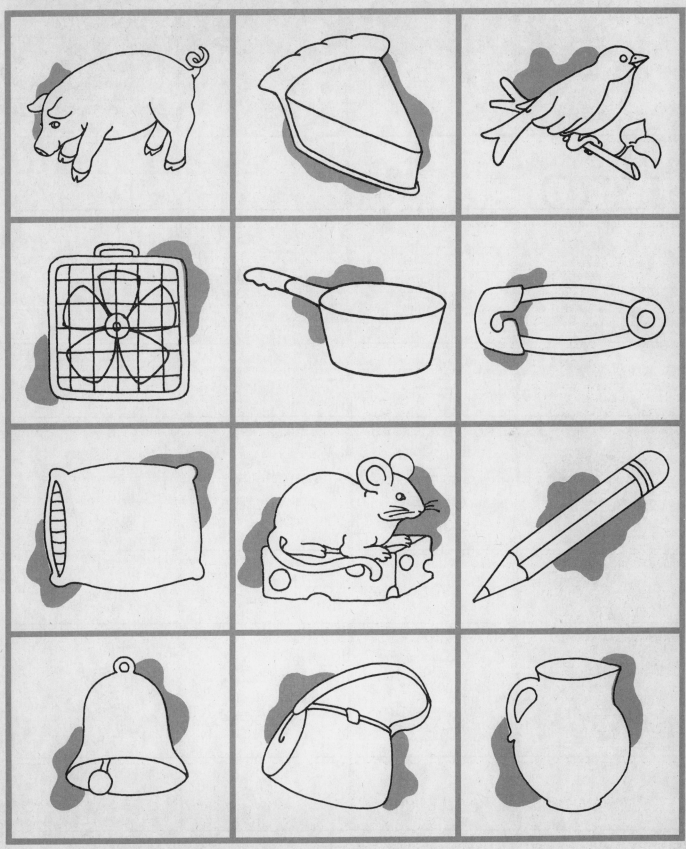

Directions: Pig begins with the sound of **P.** Color each picture whose name begins with the sound of **P.**

87

Directions: Say the name of the picture. If you hear the sound of **P** at the beginning, print **Pp** in the space below the picture. Color each picture whose name ends with the sound of **P**.

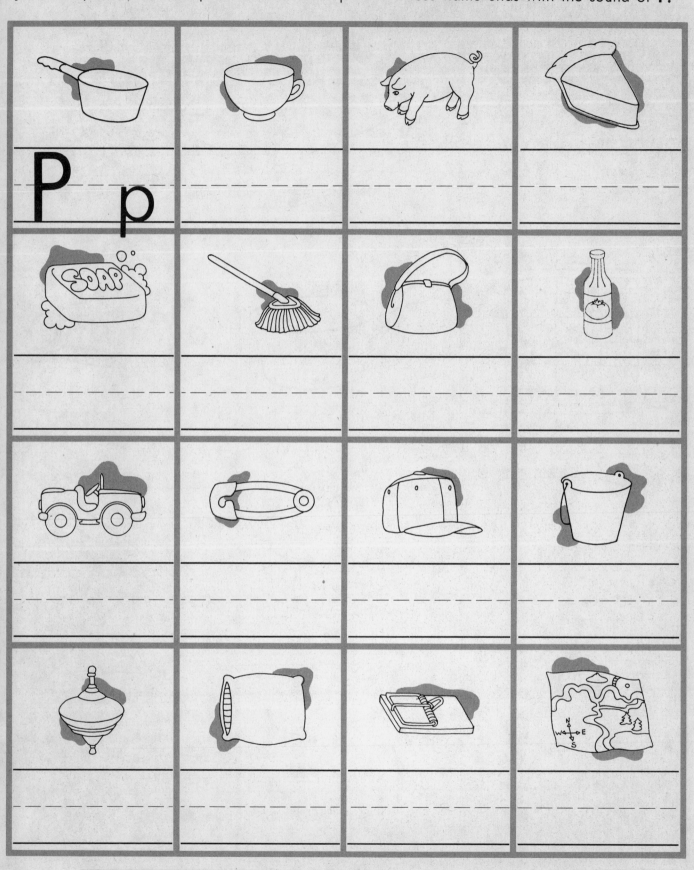

Directions: Say the name of the picture. If the name of the picture begins with the sound of **Qu,** print **Qu** in the space at the left of the picture.

We always stand side by side.

Directions: Vase begins with the sound of **V.** Say the name of the picture. If the name of the picture begins with the sound of **V,** print **Vv** in the space below the picture.

V v

Directions: In each row draw a ring around each picture whose name begins with the sound of the letter at the beginning of the row.

p				
q				
v				
p				
q				
v				

Directions: Say the name of the picture. Print the letter for the beginning sound in the box at the left. Print the letter for the ending sound in the box at the right. The first one shows you what to do.

p n			

92

LESSON 36: RECOGNIZING THE SOUND OF X

Directions: Ox ends with the sound of **X.** Color each picture whose name ends with the sound of **X.**

Directions: Ox ends with the sound of **X.** Color each picture whose name ends with the sound of **X.**

Directions: Say the name of the picture. Draw a ring around the beginning letter of the name of each picture. Color each picture whose name begins with the sound of **Y**.

Y
X
W
V
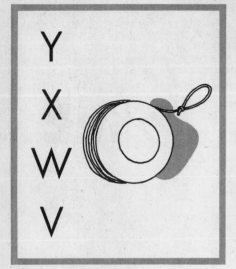

Y
X
W
V

Y
X
W
V

R
F
Y
X
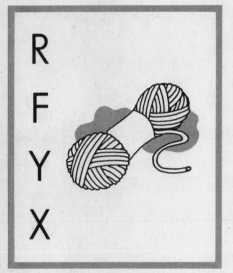

R
F
X
B

B
R
V
Y

B
R
V
Y

B
R
V
Y

B
R
V
Y

94

Directions: Say the name of the picture. Draw a ring around the beginning letter of the name of each picture. Color each picture whose name begins with the sound of **Z**.

S Z N Y

S Z X Y

X Y Z S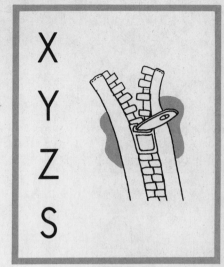

S Z N Y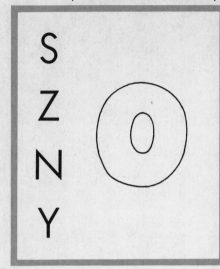

S Z N Y

S Z N Y

X Y S Z

X Y S Z

Z X Y S

Directions: Say the name of the picture. If the name begins with the sound of the letter in the circle, color the left block. If it ends with that sound, color the right block.

Directions: Say the name of the picture. Print the letter for the beginning sound. Then print the letter for the ending sound to complete the name for each picture.

a	e	u	u
a	o	e	a
o	ee	e	oa
ea	u	oo	oa

Directions: Say the name of the picture. Print the middle letter to complete the name. The first one shows you what to do.

radio	ba y le	on
vio in	wa on	spi er
tu ip	se en	ti er
gi affe	dra on	li y

Directions: Say the name of the picture. Draw a ring around the name of the vowel that you hear. The first one shows you what to do.

a e (i) o u	a e i o u	a e i o u	a e i o u
a e i o u	a e i o u	a e i o u	a e i o u
a e i o u	a e i o u	a e i o u	a e i o u

Directions: Look at the letter in the top of the box. Find the same letter in each word and draw a ring around it. The first ones show you what to do.

a				
a (ant)	cap	ax	lamp	papa	hand
	and	plant	apple	rabbit	cannot

i				
i (six)	lips	ill	gift	mitt	ring
	itself	tiptop	quilt	ticket	million

u				
u (bug)	up	duck	nuts	scrub	sunny
	puppy	under	sunset	uphill	hugs

o				
o (top)	off	mom	ox	stop	block
	pond	ribbon	socks	frost	doctor

e				
e (web)	net	egg	men	swell	bell
	camel	seven	helper	twenty	pencil

Directions: Say the name of the picture as you slide down the hill. Print its name on the line. The first ones show you what to do.

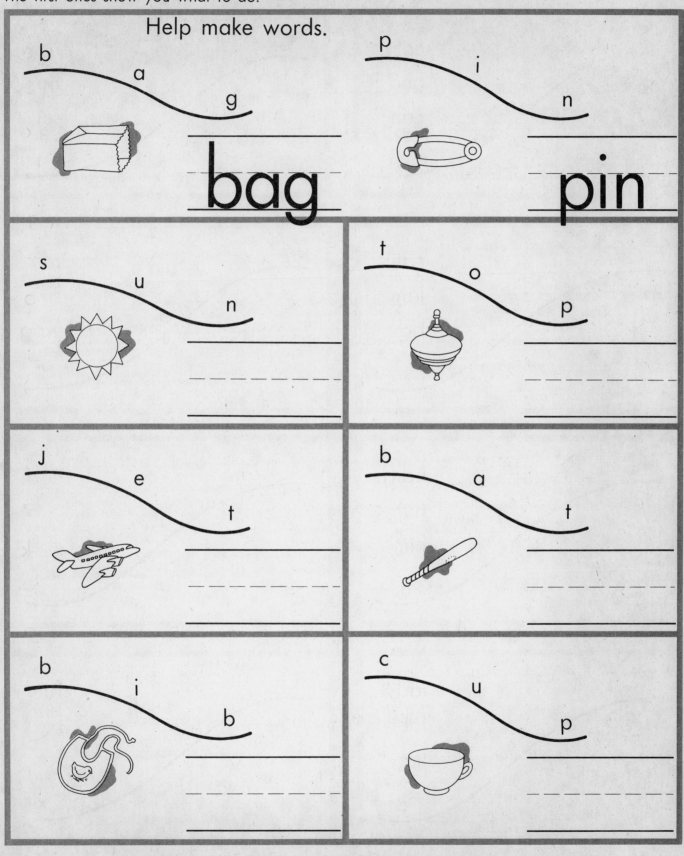

Help make words.

b a g

bag

p i n

pin

s u n

t o p

j e t

b a t

b i b

c u p

101

Directions: Draw a ring around the word that you make when you slide down the hill. Say the word. The first one shows you what to do.

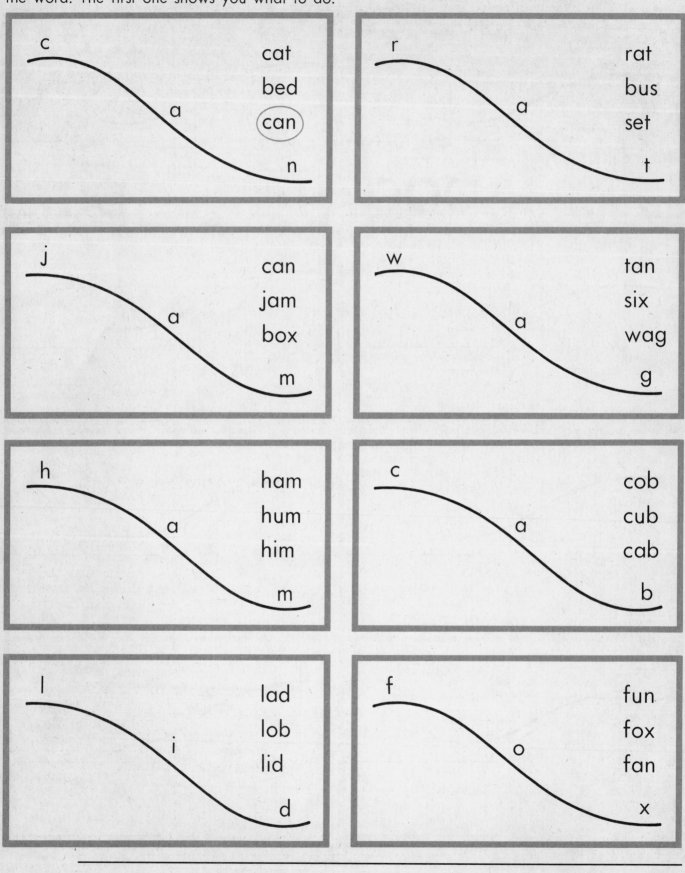

c
a
cat
bed
(can)
n

r
a
rat
bus
set
t

j
a
can
jam
box
m

w
a
tan
six
wag
g

h
a
ham
hum
him
m

c
a
cob
cub
cab
b

l
i
lad
lob
lid
d

f
o
fun
fox
fan
x

Directions: Ant has the short sound of **A.** Color each picture whose name has the short sound of **A.**

Directions: Say the names of the pictures. In each row color the pictures that have rhyming names.

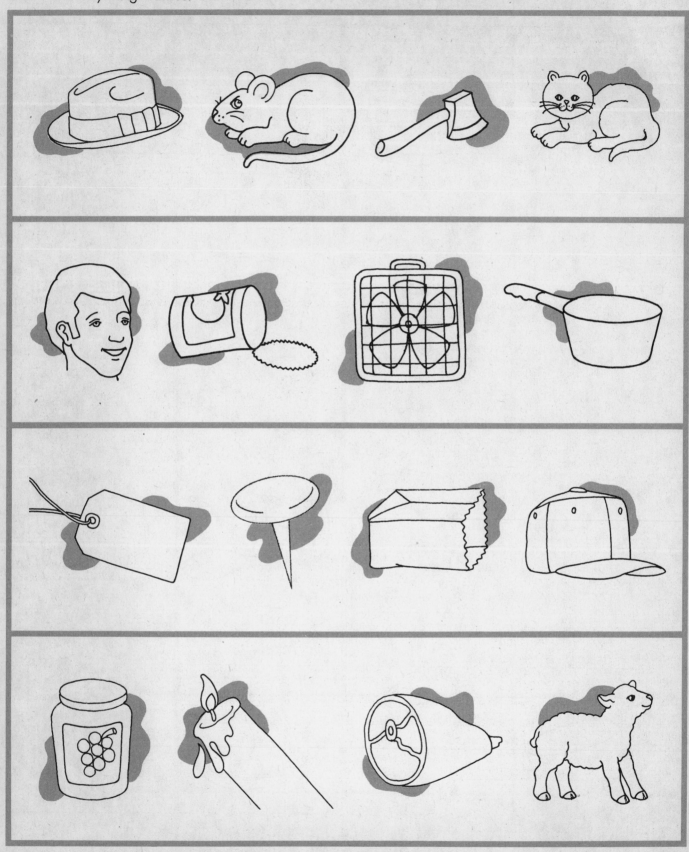

Directions: Draw a ring around the word that is the name of the picture.
Color all the pictures.

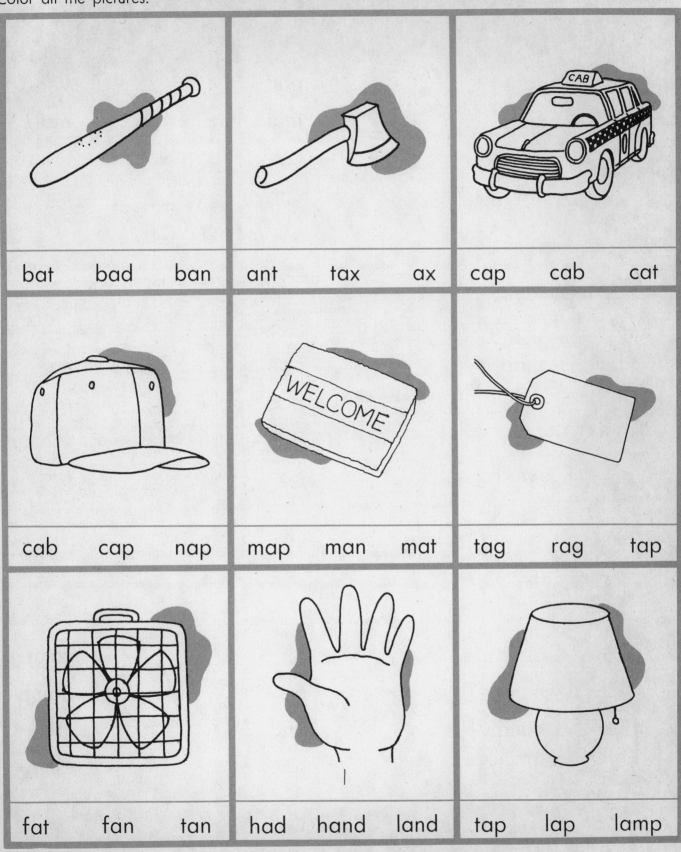

bat bad ban	ant tax ax	cap cab cat
cab cap nap	map man mat	tag rag tap
fat fan tan	had hand land	tap lap lamp

Directions: Draw a ring around the word that is the name of the picture.

Directions: Say the name of the picture. Draw a ring around its name.

tag
bag
wag
bad

nab
mat
cab
cat

van
mat
man
ran

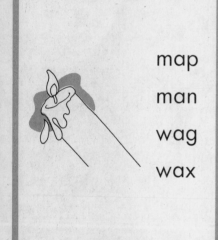

map
man
wag
wax

pan
pad
pal
pat

cat
rat
ran
rag

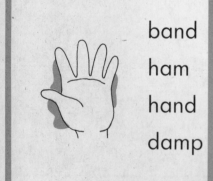

band
ham
hand
damp

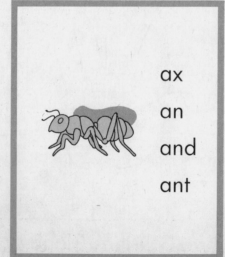

ax
an
and
ant

camp
damp
land
lamp

Directions: Look at the picture. Read the sentence that is started for you. Draw a ring around the word that completes it, and print it on the line.

	Ann has a _____ .	bat bad ban
	Dan has Dad's _____ .	had bat hat
	Pam has a fat _____ .	mat cap cat
	The cat can nab a _____ .	cat rat sat
	Max had a tan _____ .	can rap cap
	Pass Max a _____ .	pal pad pan

Directions: Say the name of the picture. Print the beginning and ending consonants on the line below the picture.

a	a	a	a
a	a	a	a
a	a	a	a
a	a	a	a

Directions: Draw a ring around the word that will complete each sentence, and print it on the line. Read the sentence to be sure that it makes sense.

Val had a _____ .	nab nan nap
Jack can pass the _____ .	jam jag jab
Nat ran past an _____ .	am ant and
Nan has a sad _____ .	cab cap cat
Sam has a bad _____ .	has hand had
Pat had a pal at _____ .	cap camp cast
Dan ran _____ .	lamp land last
Jan can hand Sam the _____ .	has ham had
Mac can pack a bag _____ .	fan fact fast

Directions: Print the name of each picture on the line below the picture.

Directions: Six has the short sound of **I**. Color each picture whose name has the short sound of **I**.

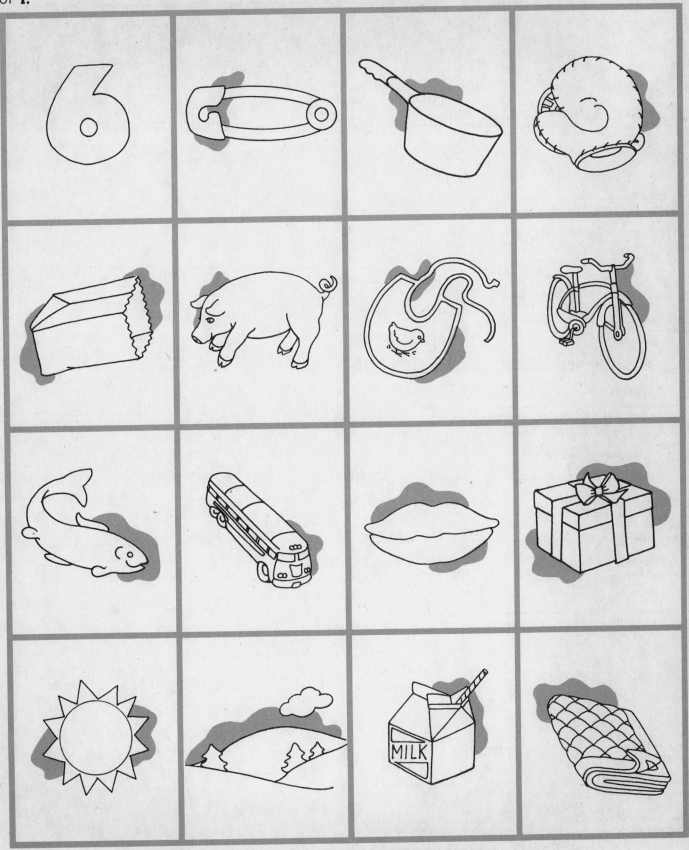

III

Directions: Say the names of the pictures. In each row color the pictures that have rhyming names.

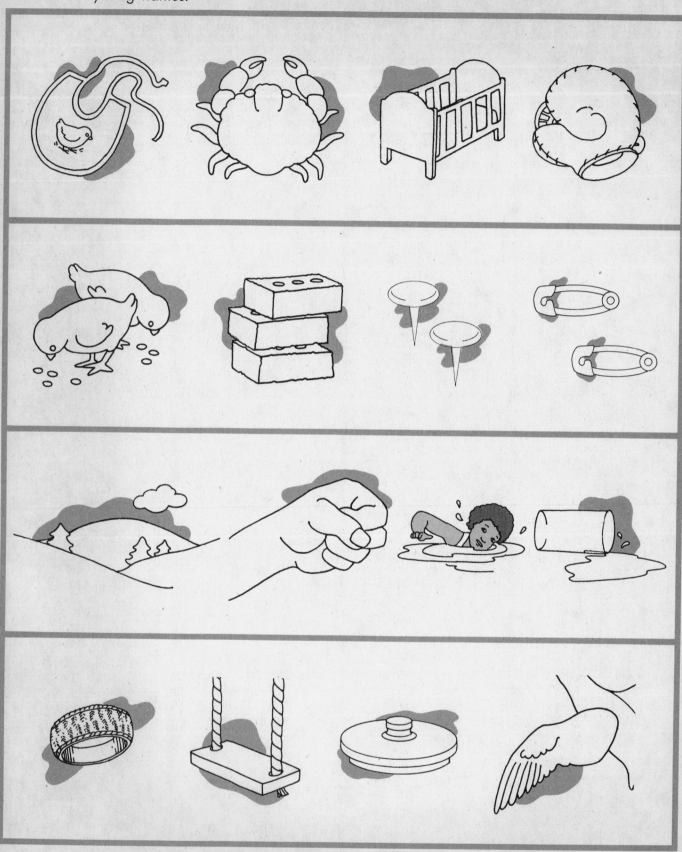

Directions: Draw a ring around the word that is the name of the picture. Color all the pictures.

six sax mix	dig big pig	hid lid lad
bin pin pan	bib bid bad	fill hill bill
mill mat mitt	rink sank sink	will milk wilt

Directions: Say the name of the picture. Draw a ring around its name.

pit
pig
gap
gag

fill
bill
hill
hid

milk
mill
will
wick

silk
sits
sank
sink

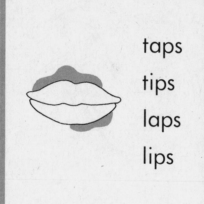

taps
tips
laps
lips

quack
quit
quilt
quick

fast
fist
fix
fill

lift
gift
sift
figs

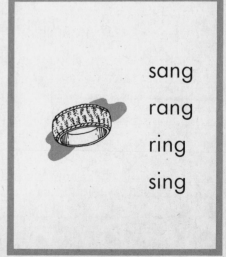

sang
rang
ring
sing

114

Directions: Look at the picture. Read the sentence that is started for you. Draw a ring around the word that completes it, and print it on the line.

	_____ - - - - - - - - - - - Tim sips the _____ .	silk milk mill
	_____ - - - - - - - - - - - Liz has a tan _____ .	wink wag wig
	_____ - - - - - - - - - - - Jim hid the pan _____ .	lid lad lip
	_____ - - - - - - - - - - - The list has six _____ .	quilt gills gifts
	_____ - - - - - - - - - - - Sid will win a _____ .	pit pig pick
	_____ - - - - - - - - - - - Kim lit the wick in the _____ .	damp lamp limp

115

Directions: Say the name of the picture. Print the beginning and ending consonants on the line below the picture.

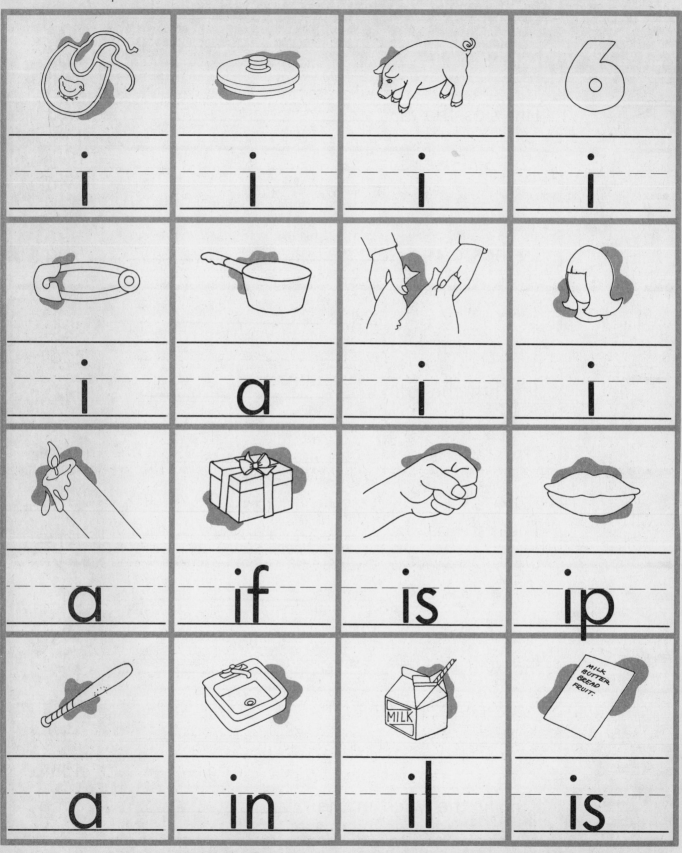

i   i   i   i

i   a   i   i

a   if   is   ip

a   in   il   is

Directions: Draw a ring around the word that will complete each sentence, and print it on the line. Read the sentence to be sure that it makes sense.

Jill has the big _____ .	lid / lick / lit
Liz hid in a sand _____ .	pig / pin / pit
The ax will fit in Sid's _____ .	kid / kit / kiss
Jan will fix the rip in the _____ .	quit / quick / quilt
The rat sank in the _____ .	sad / sag / sand
Rick will pass the _____ .	mid / mitt / miss
The mitt can fit _____ .	Dick / Did / Digs
If Jim is ill, Kim will miss _____ .	hit / hill / him
Tim will fill the big _____ .	bat / bag / band

Directions: Print the name of each picture on the line below the picture.

_____	_____	_____
_____	_____	_____
_____	_____	_____
_____	_____	_____

Directions: Look at the picture and the word below the picture. Print the missing vowel to complete the name of each picture.

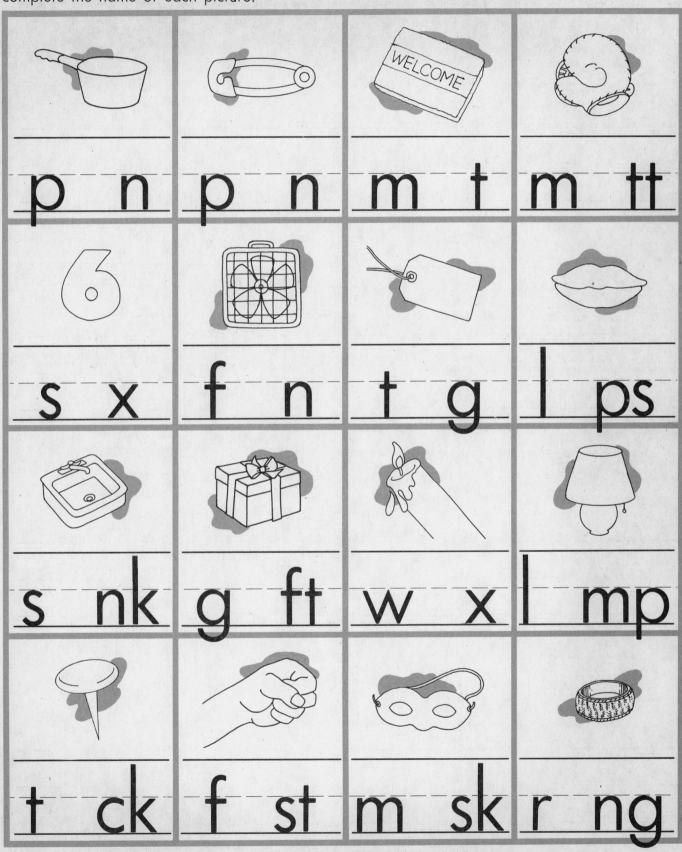

p n	p n	m t	m tt
s x	f n t	g l	p s
s nk	g ft	w x l	mp
t ck	f st	m sk	r ng

LESSON 43: REVIEWING SHORT A AND I

Directions: Color the balloon yellow if it has three rhyming short **A** words. Color the balloon red if it has three rhyming short **I** words.

Directions: Bug has the short sound of **U.** Color each picture whose name has the short sound of **U.**

Directions: Bug has the short sound of **U.** Color each picture whose name has the short sound of **U.**

Directions: Say the names of the pictures. In each row color the pictures that have rhyming names.

Directions: Draw a ring around the word that is the name of the picture.
Color all the pictures.

sup sum sun	gum gull gust	cut cap cup
sub bus sun	bag bug big	but tab tub
jug jab gag	tusk mug nuts	tuck duck buck

Directions: Say the name of the picture. Draw a ring around its name.

	dump		jab		mug
	jump		jug		mud
	pump		pug		muff
	pup		gum		milk

	rig		bid		duck
	rag		bad		buck
	rug		dub		luck
	rub		bud		tuck

	puff		dull		tank
	muff		gull		sunk
	cuff		full		run
	cut		sulk		sun

124

Directions: Look at the picture. Read the sentence that is started for you. Draw a ring around the word that completes it, and print it on the line.

	Ann ran the _____.	bus us cub
	Kim will cut the _____.	bum tub bun
	A bug bit the _____.	bug pub pup
	The pup will tug at the _____.	rut rug rig
	Big Duck can't fit in the _____.	tug tab tub
	Judd had a cup of _____.	huts nuts rugs

125

Directions: Say the name of the picture. Print the beginning and ending consonants on the line below the picture.

u	u	u	u
u	u	u	u
u	a	a	u
ul	u	uc	ut

Directions: Draw a ring around the word that will complete each sentence, and print it on the line. Read the sentence to be sure that it makes sense.

Sis will hug Bud's _____.	pup punt pump
The pig dug in the _____.	must mud muff
Pat and Gus hid in the _____.	hut hug hum
Jump up and hand Pam a _____.	bus bum bun
Gus has a big pack of _____.	gull gust gum
Judd sips his cup of _____.	milk mill mist
A gust of wind hit the _____.	hid hip hill
Nan will pump gas _____ into the tank of the _____.	bug bus bun
The pup can run _____ fast and _____.	just junk jump

Directions: Print the name of each picture on the line below the picture.

LESSON 46: REVIEWING SHORT A, I, U

Directions: Look at the picture and the word below the picture. Print the missing vowel to complete the name of each picture.

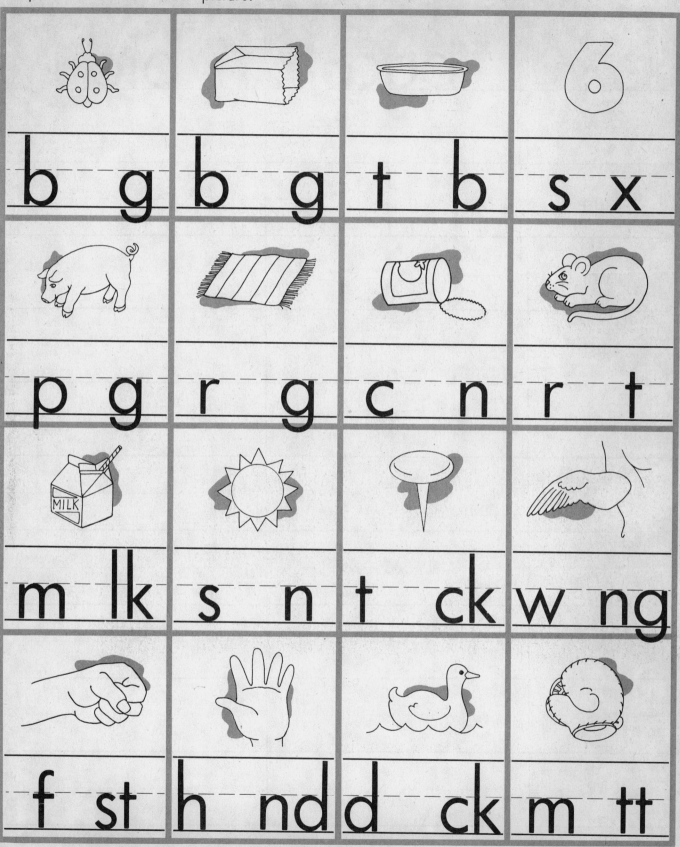

b _ g	b _ g	t _ b	s _ x
p _ g	r _ g	c _ n	r _ t
m _ lk	s _ n	t _ ck	w _ ng
f _ st	h _ nd	d _ ck	m _ tt

Directions: Look at the vowel in the word at the beginning of the row. Change it to **a** and print the new word in the space. Then change it to **i**. The first one shows you what to do.

bud	bad	bid
hut		
hum		
fun		
bug		
but		
rug		
suck		
tuck		
must		
lump		

Directions: Top has the short sound of **O.** Color each picture whose name has the short sound of **O.**

Directions: Say the names of the pictures. In each row color the pictures that have rhyming names.

Directions: Draw a ring around the word that is the name of the picture.
Color all the pictures.

| top | pot | pod | box | fox | fog | log | dog | lot |

| nap | map | mop | cat | cut | cot | hat | hot | hit |

| dug | dig | dog | rid | rod | sod | dill | dull | doll |

Directions: Say the name of the picture. Draw a ring around its name.

bib
bob
fox
box

hop
tip
top
tap

pop
pup
pad
dog

cat
cot
cut
sob

ax
ox
six
mix

lock
sack
tack
sock

rack
dock
rock
tock

lick
lock
luck
lost

pant
pink
fond
pond

Directions: Look at the picture. Read the sentence that is started for you. Draw a ring around the word that completes it, and print it on the line.

	Dot is fond of _____ .	dogs docks dolls
	Todd's gift to Don is in a _____ .	fox box boss
	A big log just hit the _____ .	rock sock rack
	Bob will lift the dog off the _____ .	lock log lost
	Val and Kim jog to the _____ .	fond pod pond
	Rob will toss his socks on the _____ .	got cot cat

135

Directions: Say the name of the picture. Print the beginning and ending consonants on the line below the picture.

O	O	O	O
O	O	O	O
O	O	O	on
OC	OC	OC	O

Directions: Draw a ring around the word that will complete each sentence, and print it on the line. Read the sentence to be sure that it makes sense.

The pop in the cup is _____.	hot hog hop
Big Bug hops on and off the _____.	lost lop log
Don will lock the big _____.	bob bog box
Nan will toss the ring to _____.	romp Ron rot
Ross lost his _____.	soft socks sod
The dog is not _____.	loft lock lost
Mom will jog to the top of the _____.	hill hid hint
Dot sat on a log at the _____.	pomp pond pock
Tom's dog will romp on the soft _____.	mum muss mud

Directions: Print the name of each picture on the line below the picture.

Directions: Look at the picture and the word below the picture. Print the missing vowel to complete the name of each picture.

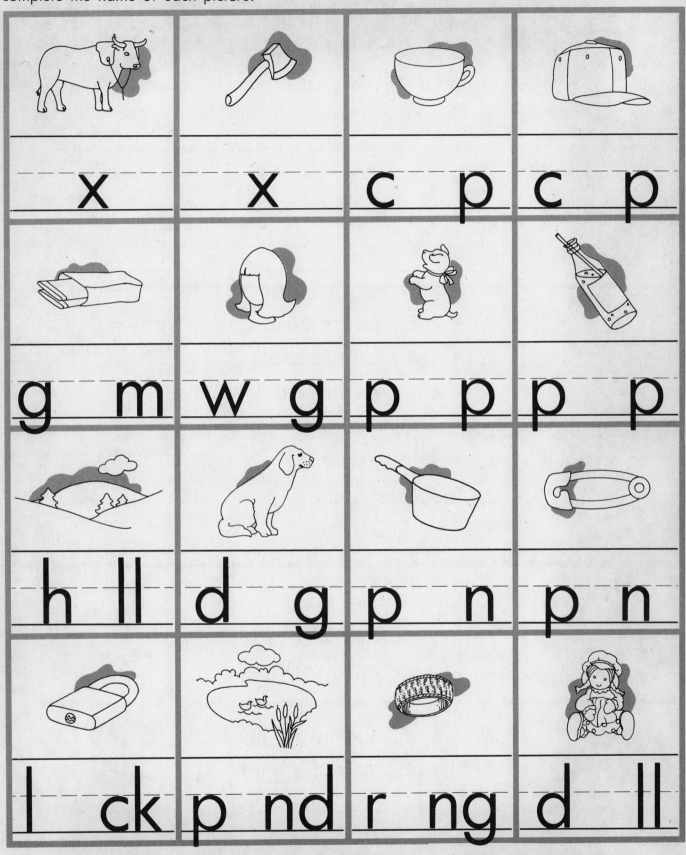

Directions: Look at the pictures. Read the sentences. Print the number of the sentence that tells about the picture in the circle below each picture. The first one shows you what to do.

1. Dot has a top.
2. Dot has pop.
3. Dot has a pup.

③

○

1. It is hot.
2. It is a ham.
3. It is a hat.

○

○

1. A cat is in the box.
2. A cat is on the rock.
3. A cat is on the mat.

○

○

1. Todd has his cap.
2. Todd has a cup.
3. Todd has a can.

○

○

1. Tim sat on a box.
2. Tim sat on a big log.
3. Tom sat on a rock.

○

○

1. The pig dug in the mud.
2. The dog is in the mud.
3. The big dog jumps up.

○

○

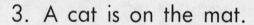

140

LESSON 50: RECOGNIZING SHORT E

Directions: Web has the short sound of **E.** Color each picture whose name has the short sound of **E.**

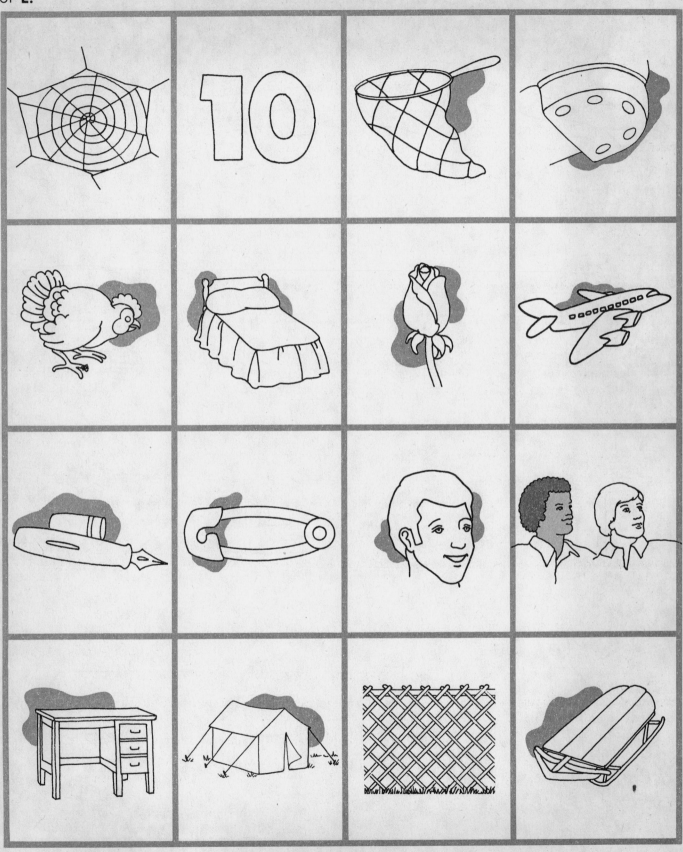

141

Directions: Say the names of the pictures. In each row color the pictures that have rhyming names.

Directions: Draw a ring around the name of the picture. Color all the pictures.

bed fed led	bill bull bell	tan ten tin
met net set	west wet web	jet pet jell
went man men	leg egg beg	ten tent bent

Directions: Say the name of the picture. Draw a ring around its name.

jot
jet
jest
just

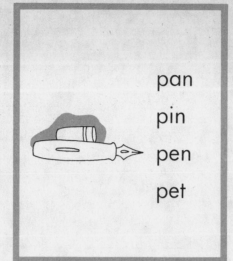

pan
pin
pen
pet

bed
bad
bid
bud

sob
nab
mob
web

will
well
west
went

felt
best
bell
belt

lent
sent
tent
tell

desk
disk
dusk
less

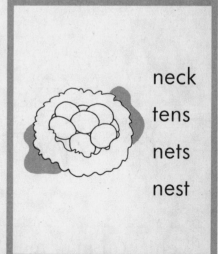

neck
tens
nets
nest

Directions: Look at the picture. Read the sentence that is started for you. Draw a ring around the word that completes it, and print it on the line.

	_____ - - - - - - - - Deb will lend Bess a _____ .	pen den pet
	_____ - - - - - - - - The ten men will rent a _____ .	get pet jet
	_____ - - - - - - - - A big rock fell in the _____ .	web well west
	_____ - - - - - - - - Ben felt the hen peck his left _____ .	beg leg peg
	_____ - - - - - - - - His pet hen left its _____ .	net neck nest
	_____ - - - - - - - - Jess will mend a rip in the _____ .	tend ten tent

Directions: Say the name of the picture. Print the beginning and ending consonants on the line below the picture.

e	i	e	e
e	e	e	e
e	e	es	es
en	le	es	el

146

Directions: Draw a ring around the word that will complete each sentence, and print it on the line. Read the sentence to be sure that it makes sense.

Ed hung a bell on the neck of his _____ .	doc dog dot
Peg and Meg fed the pigs in the _____ .	pen pep pet
Ted had a red quilt on his _____ .	beg belt bed
Bev fell in the pond and got _____ .	wed wet web
The sun sets in the _____ .	west well went
Get Kent a big desk to fit _____ .	hid hit him
The man let Bess sit at his _____ .	dell desk dent
The last man on the list is the _____ .	bell best bent
Yes, Deb has the best belts to _____ .	set sent sell

Directions: Print the name of each picture on the line below the picture.

Directions: Say the name of the picture. Print the name of each picture on the line below the picture.

Directions: Draw a ring around the sentence that tells about the picture.

Tad has a fan.

Todd has fun.

The cat's bed is in the sun.

The red bud is in the sun.

Kim's pet is not in the pen.

Jan adds nuts to the pan.

Dot met Bev at the dock.

Deb pets Red, the pet duck.

The man left the cab at the inn.

The men lift the keg to fix it.

Miss Keck rang a bell on the desk.

Vic fed the big tan hen.

Directions: Cake has the long sound of **A.** Color each picture whose name has the long sound of **A.**

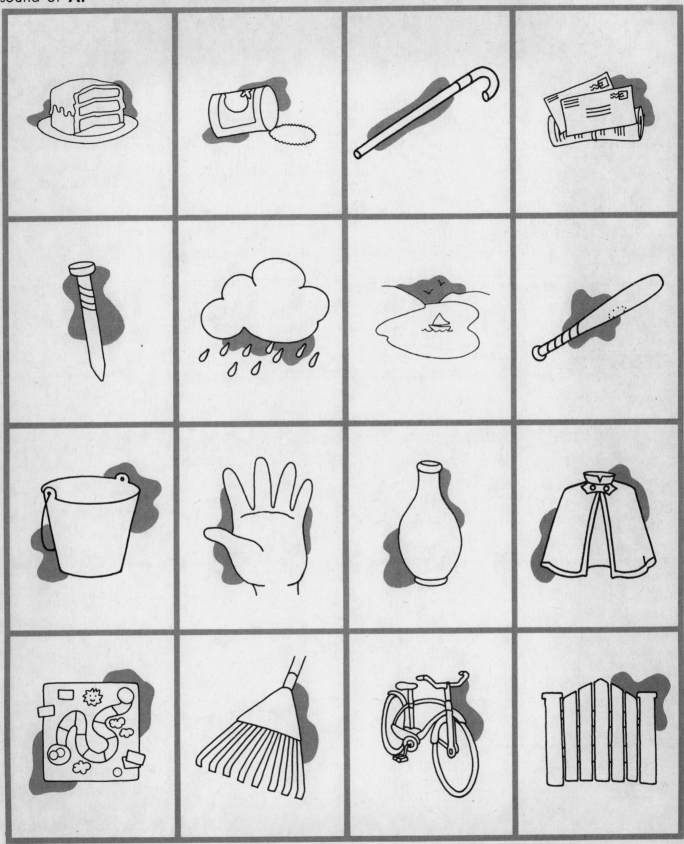

Directions: Cake has the long sound of **A.** Color each picture whose name has the long sound of **A.**

Directions: Say the names of the pictures. In each row color the pictures
that have rhyming names.

Directions: Draw a ring around the name of the picture. Color all the pictures.

pal pail bale	sack sake rake	cane can came
case cap cape	gave game pave	made mail lame
gate tape date	cave save vase	take bake lake

Directions: Say the name of the picture. Draw a ring around its name.

cake
make
cane
sake

bake
cape
cap
back

mail
nail
lane
lame

main
man
ran
rain

rack
rake
sack
sake

tape
tap
pat
bait

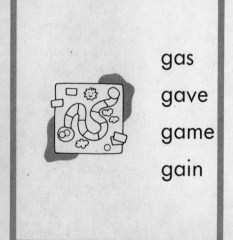
gas
gave
game
gain

cave
save
vane
vase

ate
ape
aim
am

Directions: Say the name of the picture. If you hear a short-vowel sound, color the box with S in it. If you hear a long-vowel sound, color the box with L in it.

S	L	S	L	S	L	S	L

S	L	S	L	S	L	S	L

S	L	S	L	S	L	S	L

155

Directions: Help Dan and Cass find short-vowel words in the top two exercises. Help Jane and Dave find long-vowel words at the bottom. Draw a ring around each one you find.

Dan

bag	fade	six	top	bake
jail	sun	bed	lame	cat

Cass

game	hen	dog	wade	mop
bus	maze	gain	mitt	hand

Jane

mad	gave	wait	late	sat
pale	pal	sail	name	nap

Dave

at	ate	rain	dam	tail
made	safe	tap	wake	Jan

Directions: Say the name of the picture. Draw a ring around its name.

rat rate	pane pan	tap tape
can cane	can cane	mate mat
cape cap	cape cap	man mane
hat hate	pal pail	ran rain

LESSON 55: RECOGNIZING LONG A

Directions: Look at the picture. Read the sentence that is started for you. Draw a ring around the word that completes it, and print it on the line.

	Dave will bake a _____ .	rake cake sake
	Kate will wade in the _____ .	lake pale late
	Dad laid a nail on a _____ .	bun fox box
	Mom made Jane a red _____ .	cap cape pave
	Gail gave the cap to an _____ .	ate ale ape
	Dale, tape the rip in the _____ .	less sell sail

Directions: Say the name of the picture. Print the missing consonants on the line below the picture.

a **e**	**a**	a **e**	a **e**
a e	a **e**	**a**	a **e**
a e	a **e**	**ai**	**a**
a	a **ai**	**ai**	**ai**

LESSON 55: RECOGNIZING LONG A

Directions: Draw a ring around the word that will complete each sentence, and print it on the line. Read the sentence to be sure that it makes sense.

It is safe to wade in the _____ .

| bag |
| bay |
| band |

Ray will take us to the _____ .

| late |
| lame |
| lake |

Dave will take a can of _____ .

| bail |
| bait |
| bake |

Kate went to the gate to get the _____ .

| main |
| make |
| mail |

Rex had paint on his _____ .

| take |
| tail |
| tame |

Kay had to wait at the _____ .

| gate |
| gain |
| gave |

It is the last day to pay the _____ .

| big |
| bill |
| bit |

The rain made the game _____ .

| land |
| lane |
| late |

It is fun to play the _____ .

| gain |
| game |
| gave |

160

Directions: Color the balloon blue if it has three rhyming long **A** words. You may choose any other color for the other balloons.

game
tame
name

same
came
ape

base
vase
case

gave
cave
ate

vane
aim
save

sail
lame
rail

tape
nape
cape

cake
rake
lake

take
jade
bait

gate
date
late

rain
gain
pain

nail
mail
pail

babe
fake
fade

raid
mate
made

cane
lane
mane

Directions: Print the name of each picture on the line below the picture.

Directions: Kite has the long sound of **I**. Color each picture whose name has the long sound of **I**.

Directions: Say the names of the pictures. In each row color the pictures that have rhyming names.

Directions: Draw a ring around the name of the picture. Color all the pictures.

mine nine vine	dive dine dime	pin pie pine
pine nine pin	bite bike kite	fine fire five
tie ride tire	vine nine rise	bite kite tile

165

Directions: Say the name of the picture. Draw a ring around its name.

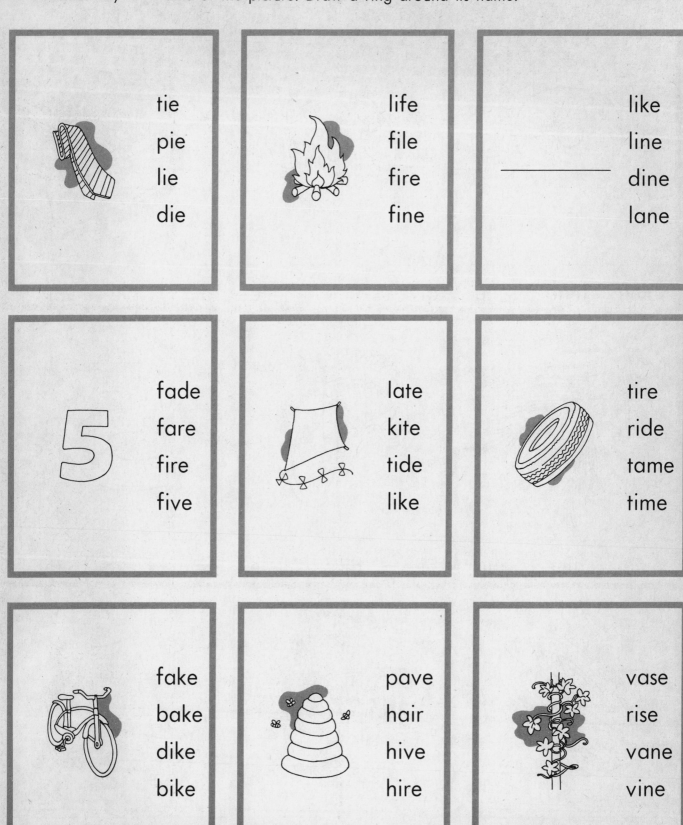

tie
pie
lie
die

life
file
fire
fine

like
line
dine
lane

fade
fare
fire
five

late
kite
tide
like

tire
ride
tame
time

fake
bake
dike
bike

pave
hair
hive
hire

vase
rise
vane
vine

Directions: Say the name of the picture. If you hear a short-vowel sound, color the box with S in it. If you hear a long-vowel sound, color the box with L in it.

S	L	S	L	S	L	S	L

S	L	S	L	S	L	S	L

S	L	S	L	S	L	S	L

167

Directions: Say the name of the picture. Draw a ring around its name.

kit kite	van vane	lid lied
dim dime	pin pine	pin pine
pan pain	cap cape	cap cape
ran rain	rip ripe	rid ride

Directions: Look at the picture. Read the sentence that is started for you. Draw a ring around the word that completes it, and print it on the line.

	Kim made a big red _____ .	tide bite kite
	Liz got a nail in the _____ .	tire time bite
	You may take a bite of Tim's _____ .	tie pie lie
	Dale can ride to the game on his _____ .	kite bake bike
	You must pay a dime for a pack of _____ .	mug gum rug
	I met nine men on the way to the _____ .	five fire fine

Directions: Say the name of the picture. Print the missing consonants on the line below the picture.

i e	i	i e	i e
___	i e	i e	i e
i e	i e	i e	i
ip	i e	i	i e

170

Directions: Draw a ring around the word that will complete each sentence, and print it on the line. Read the sentence to be sure that it makes sense.

Mike will hide in the _____.	ham hay hand
Kim rides five miles a _____.	dim dive day
Tim likes to ride his _____.	bin bite bike
Kate made a safe fire on the _____.	sand sale sake
Don's red tie is just like _____.	miss mill mine
Ed and Jake will ride to the _____.	game get gave
Will you hire Pat to fix the _____?	pill pipe pink
Dave will dive into the lake for a _____.	dime dine died
Gail will wipe the mud off the _____.	time tide tire

Directions: Print the name of each picture on the line below the picture.

Directions: Uniform has the long sound of **U.** Color each picture whose name has the long sound of **U.**

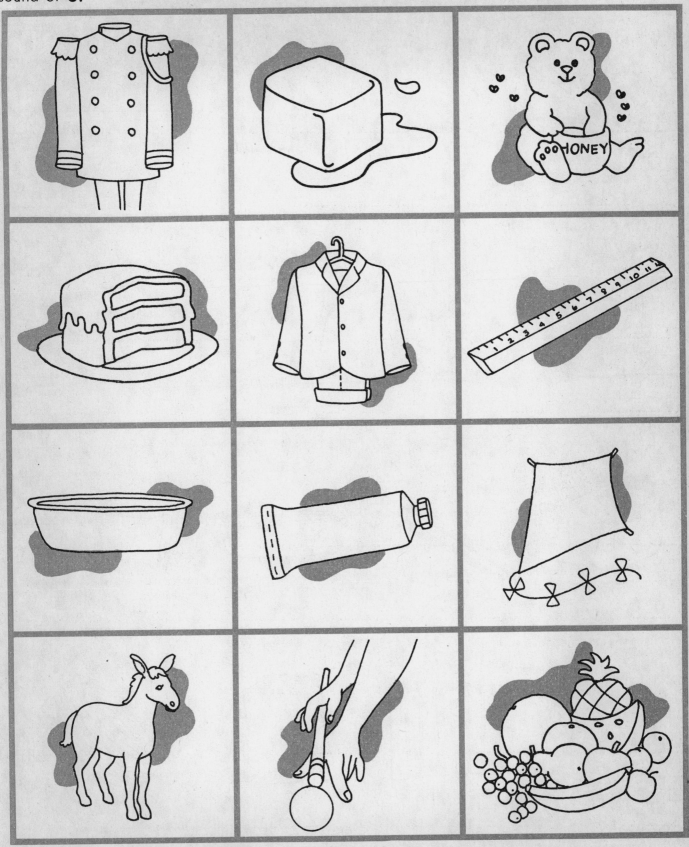

Directions: Say the names of the pictures. In each row color the pictures that have rhyming names.

Directions: Draw a ring around the name of the picture. Color all the pictures.

rule	rude	rug	cute	cub	cube	cup	cub	cube

tug	tube	tub	tune	tube	tub	due	Sue	cue

five	fire	tire	rule	mule	mute	use	sit	suit

Directions: Say the name of the picture. Draw a ring around its name.

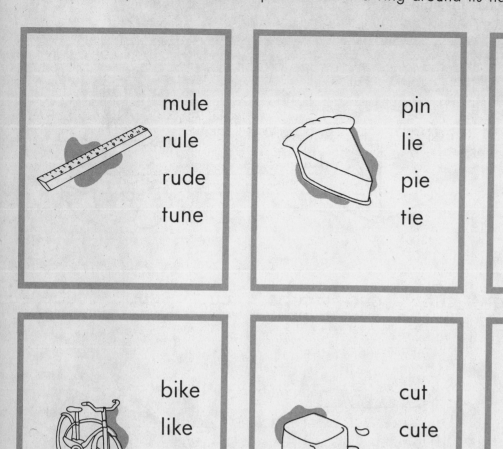

mule
rule
rude
tune

pin
lie
pie
tie

tune
lube
tub
tube

bike
like
dike
bite

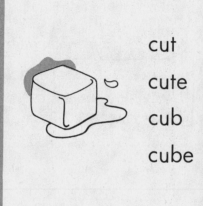

cut
cute
cub
cube

ran
rain
mine
rate

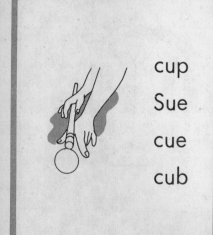

cup
Sue
cue
cub

mute
lure
mule
rule

tug
use
sit
suit

Directions: Say the name of the picture. If you hear a short-vowel sound, color the box with S in it. If you hear a long-vowel sound, color the box with L in it.

S	L	S	L	S	L	S	L

S	L	S	L	S	L	S	L

S	L	S	L	S	L	S	L

177

Directions: Color red each balloon that contains three rhyming words and long **U**. Color yellow any other balloons that contain three rhyming words.

178

Directions: Say the name of the picture. Draw a ring around its name.

tub tube	tub tube	pin pine
dim dime	cap cape	cap cape
cub cube	cub cube	rid ride
ran rain	duck duke	cut cute

Directions: Look at the picture. Read the sentence that is started for you. Draw a ring around the word that completes it, and print it on the line.

	Dad gave June a cute _____ .	pop pup pep
	June made Duke a red _____ .	sit tie suit
	Sue likes to ride the _____ .	lame mail mule
	Luke will lend Sue his _____ .	rule mule mug
	If you can hum a tune, I can name the _____ .	June tune nail
	Jule will use cubes of ham and the _____ .	legs begs eggs

Directions: Say the name of the picture. Print the missing consonants on the line below the picture.

u __ e	__ u	u __ e	__ i __ e
__ a __ e	u __ e	__ i __ e	__ a __ e
__ i __ e	__ u	u __ e	__ u __ e
__ u	__ u i	__ a i	u __ e

Directions: Draw a ring around the word that will complete each sentence, and print it on the line. Read the sentence to be sure that it makes sense.

The air is not _____.	pure puck puff
The fumes of the fire are _____.	bat bed bad
Dr. Pam will cure _____.	lube luck Luke
Duke fell off the _____.	must mule muck
June gave Sue a box of _____.	danes dates dares
Mom got Sue a tube of _____.	past pass paste
The game has five _____.	rules ruts rugs
Sue and Luke sang a _____.	tub tug tune
Jule will ride his bike a _____.	miss mile milk

Directions: Print the name of each picture on the line below the picture.

Directions: Print the name of each picture on the line below the picture. Color each picture whose name has the long sound of **U**.

Directions: Rose has the long sound of **O.** Color each picture whose name has the long sound of **O.**

Directions: Say the names of the pictures. In each row color the pictures that have rhyming names.

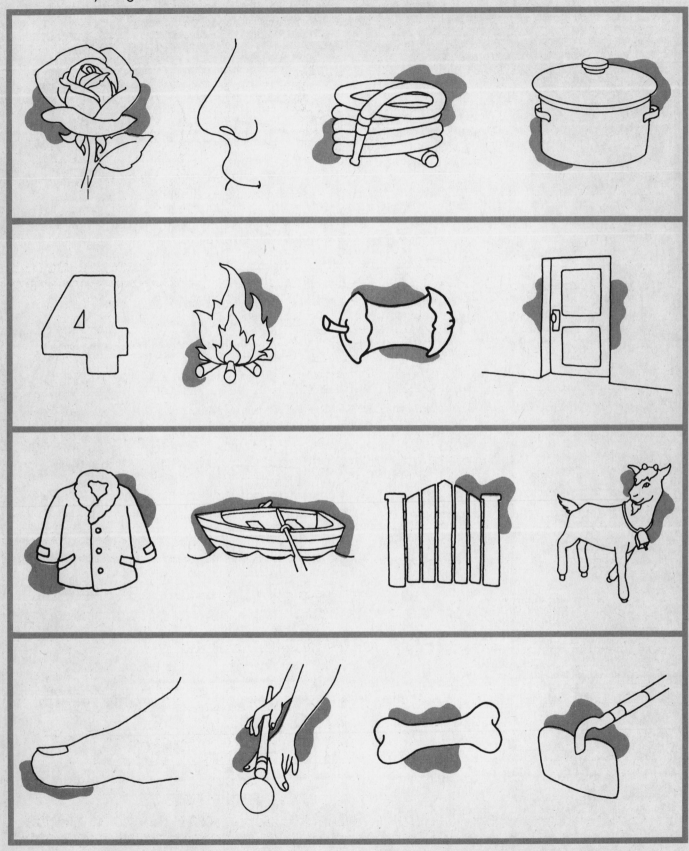

Directions: Draw a ring around the name of the picture. Color all the pictures.

ripe rope rip	rain cone cane	robe rob bore
name rose nose	sop sap soap	fair four fire
road rod ride	gate got goat	doe hoe toe

Directions: Say the name of the picture. Draw a ring around its name.

rose
nose
rise
sore

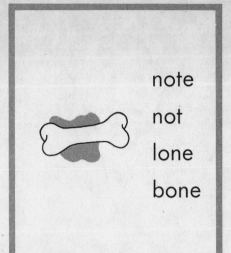

note
not
lone
bone

cot
coat
cut
cute

bait
bat
boat
bite

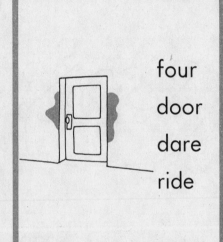

four
door
dare
ride

tail
soap
road
toad

pure
pare
ripe
rope

cue
tie
hoe
toe

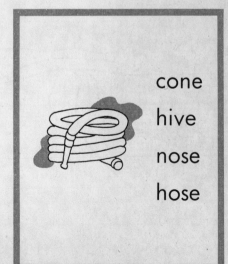

cone
hive
nose
hose

Directions: Say the name of the picture. If you hear a short-vowel sound, color the box with S in it. If you hear a long-vowel sound, color the box with L in it.

S	L	S	L	S	L	S	L

S	L	S	L	S	L	S	L

S	L	S	L	S	L	S	L

189

Directions: Say the name of the picture at the left. In the box draw a ring around each word that rhymes with the name of the picture. Draw an X on each short-vowel word.

	bone	cane	loan	line	moan
	can	Joan	tone	tune	run
	got	boat	coat	note	cute
	vote	bait	tote	quit	quote
	four	pour	dare	care	roar
	core	cure	more	sore	wore
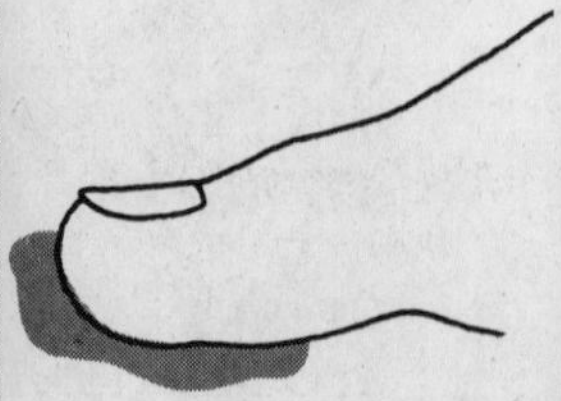	at	hoe	oat	Joe	go
	Moe	no	tie	doe	lie

190

Directions: Say the name of the picture. Draw a ring around its name.

coat cot	cot coat	mop mope
kit kite	rod road	road rod
cub cube	cub cube	rob robe
got goat	sop soap	rat rate

Directions: Look at the picture. Read the sentence that is started for you. Draw a ring around the word that completes it, and print it on the line.

	_____ - - - - - - - - - - - Joan likes to jump _____ .	rope role robe
	_____ The big goat - - - - - - - - - - takes Mom's _____ .	core coal coat
	_____ - - - - - - - - - - Bob got a bump on his _____ .	rose nose soap
	_____ - - - - - - - - - - Joe tore a hole in his _____ .	rode robe sole
	_____ Bev and Joan - - - - - - - - - - will go in the _____ .	bite bait boat
	_____ - - - - - - - - - - Moe gave Mom a red _____ .	role toe rose

Directions: Say the name of the picture. Print the missing consonants on the line below the picture.

o e	o e	o e	o
o e	oa	o	o e
oa	o	oa	oa
oa	o e	ou	on

193

Directions: Draw a ring around the word that will complete each sentence, and print it on the line. Read the sentence to be sure that it makes sense.

Dot's big toe is _____.	soap song sore
Dad will need to use the _____.	hope hoe hop
Jane wore a rose on her _____.	suit sub sun
Joe will loan his bike to _____.	joke jog Joan
It cost Moe a dime for a _____.	coal cost coke
The toad went _____ hop, hop on the way _____.	hot home hose
The dog dug a _____ big hole to hide its _____.	boss bone boat
Bob rode his bike _____ to the end of the _____.	road robe role
Rose dove into the pond to save _____.	lube luck Luke

Directions: Print the name of each picture on the line below the picture.

Directions: Print the name of each picture on the line below the picture. Color each picture whose name has the long sound of **O.**

Directions: Bee has the long sound of **E.** Color each picture whose name has the long sound of **E.**

Directions: Say the names of the pictures. In each row color the pictures that have rhyming names.

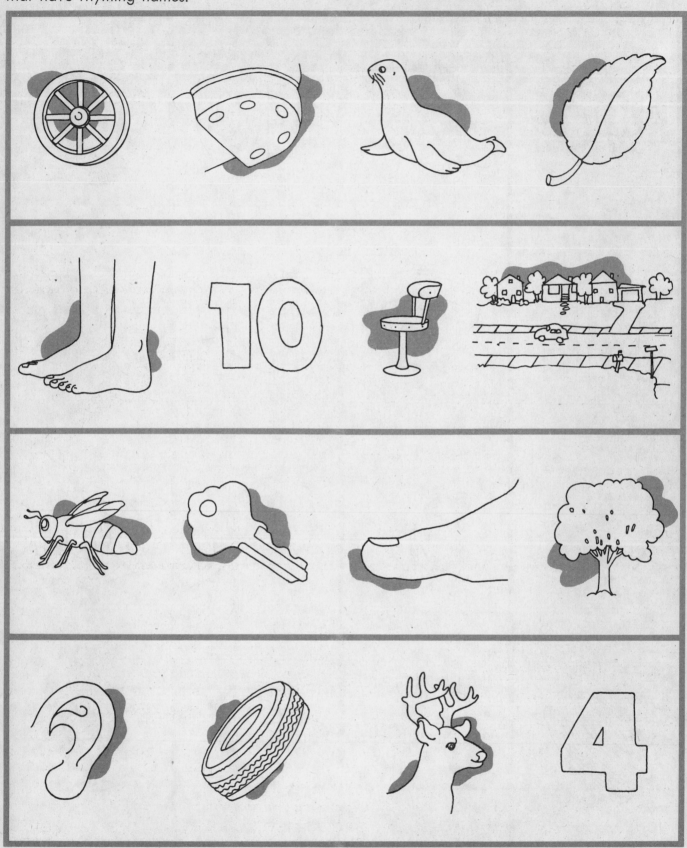

Directions: Draw a ring around the name of the picture. Color all the pictures.

| beat | feed | feet | leaf | lead | feel | fear | ear | hear |

| feel | heel | heat | see | tea | bee | real | seat | seal |

| jeep | Jean | peep | read | deer | deep | keg | see | key |

199

Directions: Say the name of the picture. Draw a ring around its name.

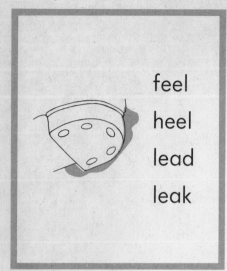

feel
heel
lead
leak

deer
read
fear
beef

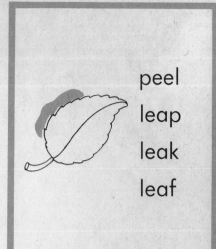

peel
leap
leak
leaf

weep
deep
jeep
jell

real
meal
seal
sell

meal
meat
neat
seat

seat
seal
teas
team

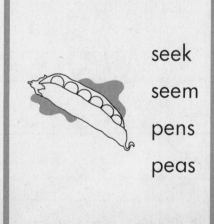

seek
seem
pens
peas

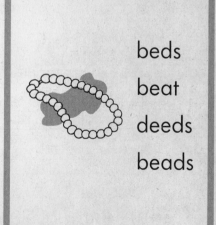

beds
beat
deeds
beads

200

Directions: Say the name of the picture. If you hear a short-vowel sound, color the box with S in it. If you hear a long-vowel sound, color the box with L in it.

S	L	S	L	S	L	S	L

S	L	S	L	S	L	S	L

S	L	S	L	S	L	S	L

Directions: Say the name of the picture at the left. In the box draw a ring around each word that rhymes with the name of the picture. Draw an X on each short-vowel word.

tea	team	see	seem	bee
bean	he	me	we	met

here	feel	men	meal	real
seal	sell	deal	deep	keep

meat	beat	bet	eat	tea
set	seat	net	heat	neat

fed	fear	near	ten	hear
rear	tear	tea	queen	deck

Directions: Say the name of the picture. Draw a ring around its name.

bed bead	met meat	kite kit
rod road	neat net	cube cub
set seat	rain ran	teen ten
dim dime	mean men	beds beads

LESSON 68: RECOGNIZING LONG E

203

Directions: Look at the picture. Read the sentence that is started for you. Draw a ring around the word that completes it, and print it on the line.

A leaf fell at Eve's _____.

fear
feel
feet

Jean lost her set of _____.

keys
keep
hear

You can hear _____ the hum of a _____.

bed
see
bee

Lee left his bean bag on the back _____.

seak
seat
teas

At a meal Ted eats beans and _____.

met
meat
team

Dee can use a key to lock the _____.

peak
peep
jeep

204

Directions: Say the name of the picture. Print the missing consonants on the line below the picture.

ee	ee	e	ee
e	ee	e	ee
ea	e	ea	en
ea	es	ea	ey

Directions: Draw a ring around the word that will complete each sentence, and print it on the line. Read the sentence to be sure that it makes sense.

The cab ran too near the _____.	jeep jeans jell
Dee and Pete will meet us _____.	heat heal here
We will be back too late for a _____.	met meal mean
The heels of Jean's feet are _____.	sock sore soap
See the man feed the _____.	seats seals seems
Deb has the best team of the _____.	yet yell year
Deb's team beat us in last week's _____.	gap game gave
Bess will get me a bag of _____.	seem sell seed
I will need lots of seed to feed the _____.	get gear geese

Directions: Print the name of each picture on the line below the picture.

Directions: Say the names of the pictures. In each row color the pictures whose names have the vowel sound shown at the left.

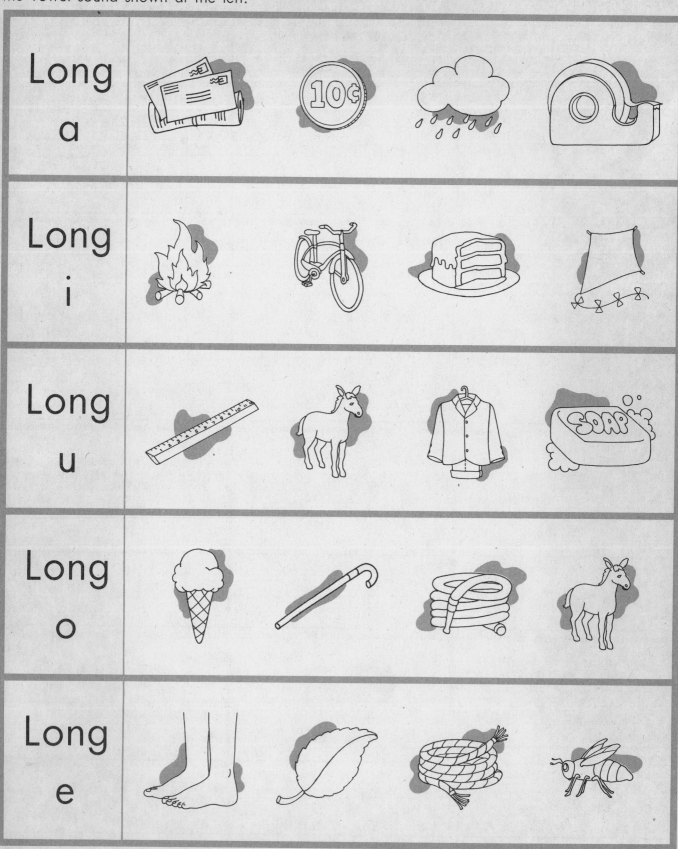

Long a

Long i

Long u

Long o

Long e

Directions: Say the names of the pictures. In each row color the pictures whose names rhyme with the word at the left.

tail

hide

lube

loan

near

Directions: Say the name of the picture at the left. In the box draw a ring around each word that has the same long vowel sound as the name of the picture. Color all the pictures.

pail	mole	rail	real	tale
mule	mail	bale	mile	sail
hike	cube	bead	hide	Mike
peak	duke	dike	like	joke
ride	coke	cute	Luke	cape
tune	beam	tube	hear	suit
fuse	pour	toad	pain	soap
hope	goat	pure	ripe	coat
feel	lube	seal	fake	jeep
beef	heat	safe	deer	life

Directions: Print the name of each picture on the line below the picture.

Directions: Print the name of each picture on the line below the picture.

211

Directions: Say the name of the picture. If you hear a short-vowel sound, color the box with S in it. If you hear a long-vowel sound, color the box with L in it.

S	L	S	L	S	L	S	L

S	L	S	L	S	L	S	L

S	L	S	L	S	L	S	L

Directions: Add a vowel to the word to make a long-vowel word. Then change the vowel in the first word to make another short-vowel word. The first one shows you what to do.

at	ate	it
hid		
cut		
rob		
pin		
hop		
tap		
cub		
met		
ran		
red		

Directions: Print the correct word in the blank to complete each sentence. Read the sentence to be sure that it makes sense.

Mike has _____ to fix the kite.	tap tape
Pat _____ home to see Dad.	ran rain
June will _____ the kite in the jeep.	hid hide
See the toad _____ up the road.	hop hope
We _____ a mile to see Bill.	rod rode
Lin will _____ us at the game.	met meet
Jean made a _____ suit for her doll.	cut cute
The dog lay on a _____ near the gate.	mat mate
On the way home _____ and Ted ate a cone.	pet Pete

Directions: Say the name of the picture in the box at the left in the row. Then color the pictures whose names begin with the same blend as the name of the picture in the box.

bride

tree

grapes

cross

215

Directions: Say the name of the picture in the box at the left in the row. Then color the pictures whose names begin with the same blend as the name of the picture in the box.

prize

frog

dress

trap

Directions: Say the name of the picture. Draw a ring around its name.

free tree	trick brick	prize cries
frog brag	cream cross	drive dress
bride braid	track train	fruit frost
dream drum	grapes grasp	crane crow

Directions: Say the name of the picture. Print the blend that you hear at the beginning of each.

_____ ab	_____ ap	_____ ide
_____ ame	_____ apes	_____ ess
_____ uck	_____ um	_____ ick
_____ ize	_____ oss	_____ og

Directions: Say the name of the picture in the box at the left in the row. Then color the pictures whose names begin with the same blend as the name of the picture in the box.

block

club

flag

glass

plant

Directions: Say the name of the picture. Draw a ring around its name.

block flock	plot plate	club bulk
brag flag	class glass	plant plan
crack clock	blade braid	float flat
plug plum	flat float	clue glue

Directions: Say the name of the picture. Print the blend that you hear at the beginning of each.

___ub	___ug	___ag
___ate	___ade	___ock
___oat	___ock	___ant
___at	___obe	___ue

Directions: Say the name of the picture in the box at the left. Then draw a ring around each picture whose name begins with the same blend as the name of the picture in the box.

sled

spade

skate

swing

snail

stop

Directions: Say the name of the picture. Draw a ring around its name.

sled slide	stops steps	spade stale
skunk spunk	spin swim	star stay
scrap scrub	smoke spoke	sweet street
square scare	green screen	stray spray

223

Directions: Say the name of the picture. Print the blend that you hear at the beginning of each.

____ ate	____ ed	____ ill
____ ing	____ ail	____ op
____ oke	____ ing	____ eet
____ ore	____ are	____ ub

Directions: Print the correct word in the blank to complete each sentence. Read the sentence to be sure that it makes sense.

Jane wore a blue dress to the _____.	play plan
Greg smiles as he greets his pals in _____.	grass class
Fran drove to the store to get green _____.	grades grapes
A crow tried to eat the fruit on the _____.	trees tries
The drum Brad got for a prize _____.	brick broke
I am glad to be the _____ in the play.	sleep star
The hill is too steep to use a _____.	sled slap
Take off the flat tire and use the _____.	spare square
Please stay and help me scrub the _____.	frost floor

Directions: Say the name of the picture. Print its name on the line below the picture.

Directions: Say the name of the picture at the left. Then draw a ring around each word with the same sound of **Y** as the picture's name. Color the picture whose name has the consonant sound of **Y**.

yes	sly	you	yoke	happy
funny	year	yeast	dry	yellow

by	lily	you	sly	my
yet	fly	Judy	cry	sky

yo-yo	baby	pony	lazy	try
Tony	yoke	yes	fry	lady

fly	twenty	yams	candy	pry
penny	yank	puppy	spy	fairy

Directions: Say the name of each picture. Draw a ring around its name. Color all the pictures.

puppy buggy	fry fly	lady baby
funny penny	pony posy	cry try
lazy lily	hairy fairy	candy sandy
spy sky	fifty twenty	sly fry

Directions: Print the correct word in the blank to complete each sentence. Read the sentence to be sure that it makes sense.

	————————	bunny
	- - - - - - - - - -	penny
I will not spend my lucky_____ .		funny

	————————	puffy
	- - - - - - - - - -	poppy
Tony's _____ is too big to carry.		puppy

	————————	sky
	- - - - - - - -	sly
You can see a jet fly in the_____ .		spy

	————————	bony
	- - - - - - - -	penny
Judy will try to ride the big_____ .		pony

	————————	lady
	- - - - - -	lily
Randy will try to grow a yellow_____ .		lazy

	————————	my
	- - - - - -	cry
If you take her candy, Baby will_____ .		by

LESSON 76: RECOGNIZING Y as a VOWEL

Directions: Say the name of the picture. Print its name on the line below the picture.

230

Directions: Read the words next to the picture. The ending sound of each word is like the ending sound in the picture's name. Draw a ring around each root word. The first one shows you what to do.

jumped	(pass)ed	fixed	ticked	bumped
	mixed	rocked	spanked	kissed
peeled	nailed	rained	filled	foamed
	leaned	healed	sailed	played
melted	waited	seated	heated	floated
	needed	loaded	landed	ended
reading	going	mixing	waiting	resting
	asking	telling	raining	boating

231

LESSON 77: RECOGNIZING WORD ENDINGS -ED and -ING

Directions: Print the correct word in the blank to complete each sentence. Read the sentence to be sure that it makes sense.

Sally will _____ her box kite.	fly / flying
Billy _____ to see the baby.	ask / asked
Bobby _____ to like Jimmy.	seem / seemed
Tony _____ the time by reading.	pass / passed
Mary is _____ to tell us a story.	go / going
Judy _____ a home for her pony.	need / needed
Frank will _____ to paint his boat.	try / trying
The snow _____ on the driveway.	melt / melted
It is _____ and the sky is black.	raining / rain

232

Directions: Thumb begins with the sound of **th.** Color each picture whose name begins with the sound of **th.**

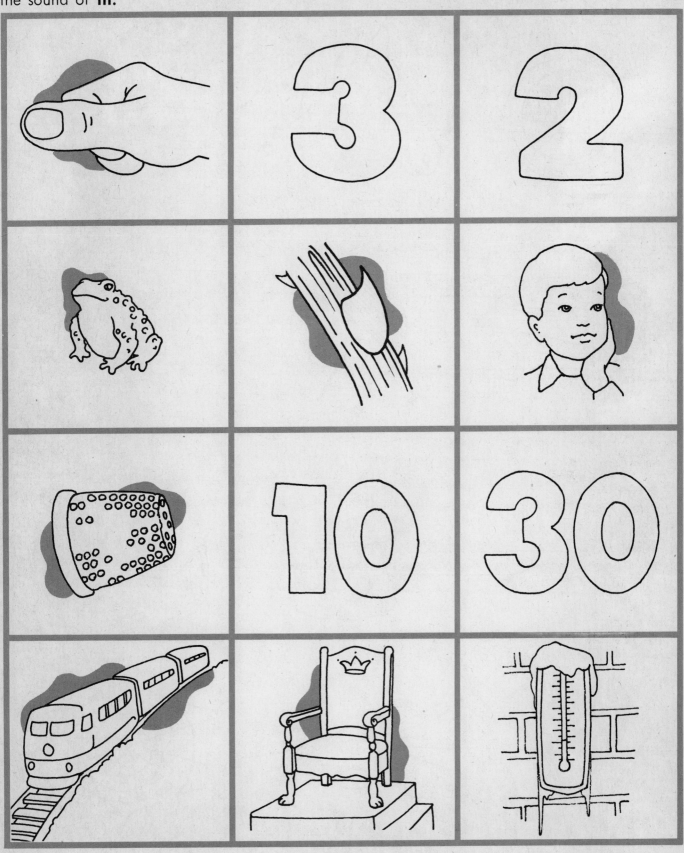

Directions: Wheel begins with the sound of **wh.** Color each picture whose name begins with the sound of **wh.**

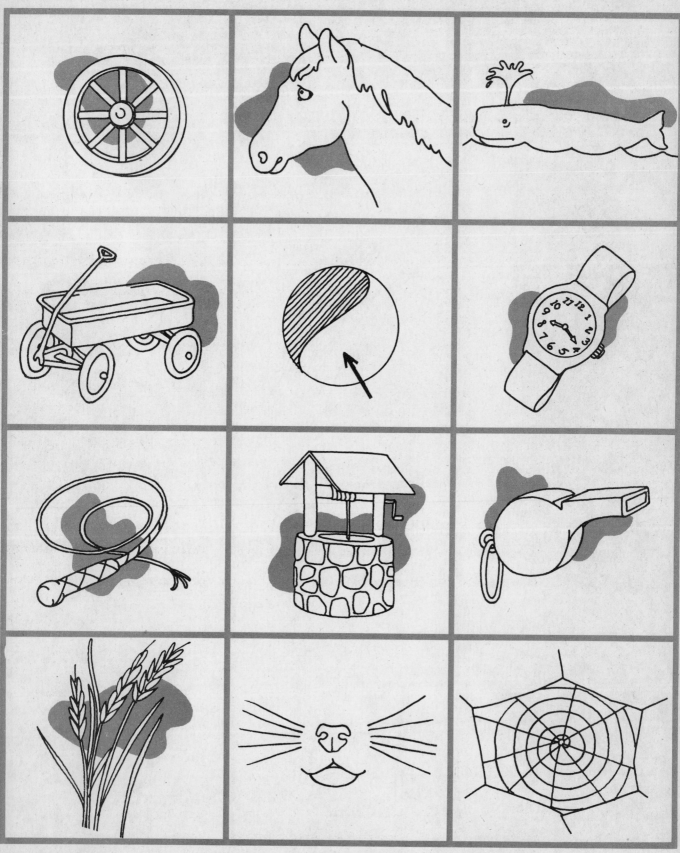

Directions: Say the name of the picture. Draw a ring around its name.

thank
think
thick
thin

wheel
wheat
why
wet

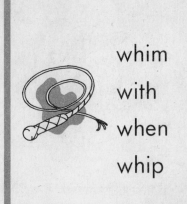

whim
with
when
whip

wait
whisk
whale
whack

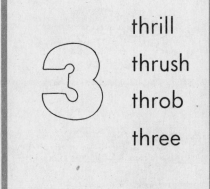

thrill
thrush
throb
three

throat
throne
thrust
these

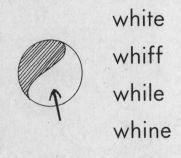

white
whiff
while
whine

trash
thug
thumb
thump

white
wheel
wheeze
wheat

LESSON 79: RECOGNIZING CONSONANT DIGRAPH SH

Directions: Sheep begins with the sound of **sh.** Color each picture whose name begins with the sound of **sh.**

Directions: Chin begins with the sound of **ch.** Color each picture whose name begins with the sound of **ch.**

Directions: Say the name of the picture. Draw a ring around its name.

ship
chip
shop
chop

chess
cheer
chair
share

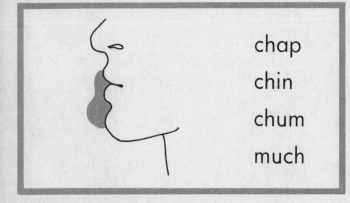

chap
chin
chum
much

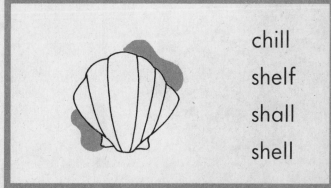

chill
shelf
shall
shell

cheat
sheet
sheep
cheap

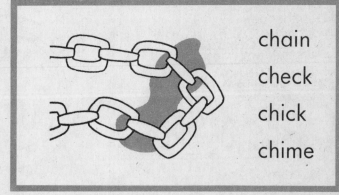

chain
check
chick
chime

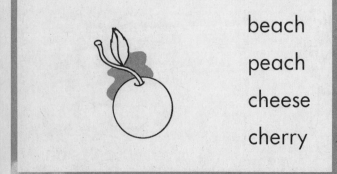

beach
peach
cheese
cherry

shape
shade
shake
shady

Directions: Say the name of the picture. Draw a ring around the consonant digraph that you hear.

th wh sh ch	th wh sh ch	th wh sh ch
th wh sh ch	th wh sh ch	th wh sh ch
th wh sh ch	th wh sh ch	th wh sh ch
th wh sh ch	th wh sh ch	th wh sh ch

Directions: Say the name of the picture. Draw a ring around the consonant digraph

239

Directions: Print the correct word in the blank to complete each sentence. Read the sentence to be sure that it makes sense.

Chad will brush his _____ well.	wish dish teeth
Beth can _____ the yellow moth.	catch pitch each
Jack has three _____ on his trike.	wells wheels wheat
Seth's kitty hides and is _____ .	shape shake shy
Why are the church _____ playing?	chins chimes chimps
_____ way did Kathy go with her puppy?	Why Which When
We flashed slides of the trip on a _____ .	sheep shell sheet
Peggy waited in the _____ for Keith.	shade share chain
Chuck will _____ cream for the cherry pie.	white wipe whip